DRUM TAPS

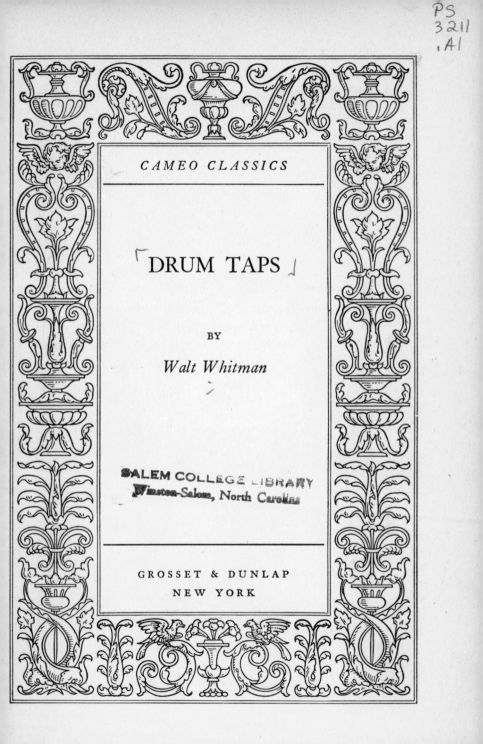

CAMEO CLASSICS

DRUM TAPS

BY

Walt Whitman

GROSSET & DUNLAP
NEW YORK

The cameo of Johann Gutenberg on the cover is from a medal produced by Anton Scharff, of Vienna, for the late Robert Hoe, from the head of the famous portrait statue of Gutenberg by the American sculptor, Ralph Goddard. Permission to use the medal was granted by the owner, William Edwin Rudge.

PRINTED IN THE UNITED STATES OF AMERICA BY
J. J. LITTLE AND IVES COMPANY, NEW YORK

INTRODUCTION

The bombardment of Fort Sumter took place a little over a month before Walt Whitman's forty-second birthday. Those long, bitter months of indecision during which the North and the South moved ever closer to the fatal clash had not been easy ones for the sensitive poet. Now the hour had come. President Lincoln had sent out his call for volunteers. Whitman's younger brother George was one of the first to respond and marched away with his Brooklyn regiment, the 51st N. Y. Volunteers. Yet the prematurely grey-haired poet remained behind in his mother's home, anxiously reading the bulletins from the front and giving expression to his emotions aroused by the beating drums and marching feet of the aroused nation through passionate poetry—the stirring poems which later appeared in *Drum Taps*.

If there were some who criticised Whitman for urging his fellows into the conflict, yet failed himself to shoulder a musket, this criticism was forgotten in the years that followed, when he dedicated his life and strength to serving his country in the humbler, less spectacular capacity of a nurse in the war hospitals in Washington.

As Richard M. Bucke says in his biography of the poet: "those who joined the ranks and fought the battles of the Republic did well; but when the world knows, as it is beginning to know, how this man, without any encouragement from without, under no compulsion, simply, without out beat of drum or any cheers of approval, went down into those immense lazar houses and devoted his days and nights, his heart and soul, and at last his health and life,

to America's sick and wounded sons, it will say that he
did even better."

In December, 1862, Walt learned that his brother, Captain George Whitman, had been wounded at the battle
of Fredericksburg, Virginia, and hurried down to find him
and nurse him back to health. At the dreary camp at Fal-
mouth, he came into contact for the first time with the
suffering, the horror and the heartbreak of war. Some of
the most poignant poems in *Drum Taps* reflect the emotions which surged through the poet during those nine
days on the banks of the Rappahannock. He followed
the wounded up to Washington, and when he saw the
thousands and thousands of young boys in blue and grey
in the hospitals and sick camps that crowded the city, he
quickly made his decision to remain and minister to the
wounded. Like his Quaker forbears, he found that his
"call" was to save life rather than take it.

All through those terrible months of battle of 1863-4
he humbly served as nurse, comforter and comrade to the
thousands of sick and dying men who were pouring into
Washington from the Virginia battlefields by every boat
and train. There was little time to write poetry, but his
thoughts often turned to *Drum Taps,* the book of verse
which he had planned back in Brooklyn when the War
first began.

In January, 1865, he wrote to a friend: "It may be
Drum Taps may come out this winter yet. . . . I am perhaps mainly satisfied with *Drum Taps* because it delivers
my ambition of the task that has haunted me, namely, to
express in a poem (and in the way I like, which is not
at all by directly stating it) , the pending action of this
Time and Land we swim in, with all their large conflicting
fluctuations of despair and hope, the shiftings, masses,
and the whirl and deafening din (yet over all, as by an

invisible hand, a definite purport and idea), with the unprecedented anguish of wounded and suffering, the beautiful young men in wholesale death and agony, everything sometimes as if blood-color and dripping blood. The book is therefore unprecedentedly sad (as these days are, are they not?), but it also has the blast of the trumpet and the drum pounds and whirrs in it, and then an undertone of sweetest comradeship and human love threads its steady thread inside the chaos and is heard at every lull and interstice thereof. Truly also, it has clear notes of faith and triumph."

The Spring of 1865 found Whitman on a few weeks' visit to the old home in Brooklyn. There was a feeling of peace in the air. He had just made the final arrangements to publish *Drum Taps* at his own expense. It was his favorite lilac-time, and the heavy scent of the blossoms came through the open windows into his rooms on that morning, when the fatal news of Lincoln's assassination flashed through the country. Grief-stricken and profoundly moved, for Lincoln had been Walt Whitman's great inspiration since the day he had come out of the West, the poet with tears blurring his eyes sat down and penned his famous Lincoln dirge, "When Lilacs Last in the Door-Yard Bloom'd" and those shorter poems, such as "O Captain! My Captain!" which coming too late to catch *Drum Taps,* already on the presses, were issued under the title *Sequel to Drum Taps.*

Bliss Perry says in his short but wonderfully understanding biography of Walt Whitman, "*Drum Taps* embody the very spirit of the civil conflict, picturing war with a poignant realism, a terrible and tender beauty, such as only the great masters of literature have been able to compass. Here the reader may still feel the electric shock of that first alarm, as the drums and bugles sound;

the ideal passion for the Flag; the sinewy tread of the
volunteer soldiery, moving so majestically that it seems as
if Democracy, or even Mankind itself, were rising from
its lethargy. Here are the pictured march and fight: the
cavalry crossing the ford, the crashing and smoking artillery, the bivouac, the field hospital at night, the vigil,
and the gaunt, ivory faces of the dead. There is no sec-
tional anger or hatred, but rather a prophesy, even in the
midst of carnage, of an ultimate reconciliation and comradeship. . . . For solemnity and power no poem in the
little volume is comparable to the threnody 'When Lilacs
Last in the Door-Yard Bloom'd,' which Swinburne, under
the spell of his first enthusiasm for Whitman, called 'the
most sonorous nocturn ever chanted in the church of the
world.' Never afterward was Whitman capable of such
sustained and deep-toned recitative, varied with lyric inter-
ludes of such pure beauty. The grief of the passing of
the great President becomes ennobled and transfigured
into a song of praise:

Come, lovely and soothing Death,
Undulate round the world, serenely arriving, arriving,
In the day, in the night, to all, to each,
Sooner or later, delicate Death.

Prais'd be the fathomless universe,
For life and joy, and for objects and knowledge curious;
And for love, sweet love—but praise! praise! praise!
For the sure-enwindng arms of cool-enfolding Death."

DRUM-TAPS

1

FIRST, O songs, for a prelude,
    Lightly strike on the stretch'd tympanum, pride
       and joy in my city,
How she led the rest to arms—how she gave the cue,
How at once with lithe limbs, unwaiting a moment, she
    sprang;
(O superb! O Manhattan, my own, my peerless!
O strongest you in the hour of danger, in crisis! O truer
    than steel!)
How you sprang! how you threw off the costumes of peace
    with indifferent hand;
How your soft opera-music changed, and the drum and
    fife were heard in their stead;
How you led to the war, (that shall serve for our prelude,
    songs of soldiers,)
How Manhattan drum-taps led.

2

Forty years had I in my city seen soldiers parading;
Forty years as a pageant—till unawares, the Lady of this
    teeming and turbulent city,
Sleepless amid her ships, her houses, her incalculable
    wealth,
With her million children around her—suddenly,

DRUM TAPS . . . .

At dead of night, at news from the south,
Incens'd, struck with clench'd hand the pavement.

A shock electric—the night sustain'd it;
Till with ominous hum, our hive at day-break pour'd out
    its myriads.
From the houses then, and the workshops, and through all
    the doorways,
Leapt they tumultuous—and lo! Manhattan arming.

3

To the drum-taps prompt,
The young men falling in and arming;
The mechanics arming, (the trowel, the jack-plane, the
    blacksmith's hammer, tost aside with precipitation;)
The lawyer leaving his office, and arming—the judge leav-
    ing the court;
The driver deserting his wagon in the street, jumping
    down, throwing the reins abruptly down on the
    horses' backs;
The salesman leaving the store—the boss, book-keeper,
    porter, all leaving;
Squads gather everywhere by common consent, and arm;
The new recruits, even boys—the old men show them how
    to wear their accoutrements—they buckle the straps
    carefully;
Outdoors arming—indoors arming—the flash of the mus-
    ket-barrels;
The white tents cluster in camps—the arm'd sentries
    around—the sunrise cannon, and again at sunset;

[2]

Arm'd regiments arrive every day, pass through the city,
    and embark from the wharves;
(How good they look, as they tramp down to the river,
    sweaty, with their guns on their shoulders!
How I love them! how I could hug them, with their
    brown faces, and their clothes and knapsacks cover'd
    with dust!)
The blood of the city up—arm'd! arm'd! the cry every-
    where;
The flags flung out from the steeples of churches, and
    from all the public buildings and stores;
The tearful parting—the mother kisses her son—the son
    kisses his mother;
(Loth is the mother to part—yet not a word does she
    speak to detain him;)
The tumultuous escort—the ranks of policemen preced-
    ing, clearing the way;
The unpent enthusiasm—the wild cheers of the crowd for
    their favorites;
The artillery—the silent cannons, bright as gold, drawn
    along, rumble lightly over the stones;
(Silent cannons—soon to cease your silence!
Soon, unlimber'd, to begin the red business;)
All the mutter of preparation—all the determin'd arming;
The hospital service—the lint, bandages, and medicines;
The women volunteering for nurses—the work begun for,
    in earnest—no mere parade now;
War! an arm'd race is advancing!—the welcome for battle
    —no turning away;
War! be it weeks, months, or years—an arm'd race is ad-
    vancing to welcome it.

[3]

4

Mannahatta a-march—and it's O to sing it well!
It's O for a manly life in the camp!

And the sturdy artillery!
The guns, bright as gold—the work for giants—to serve
    well the guns:
Unlimber them! no more, as the past forty years, for
    salutes for courtesies merely;
Put in something else now besides powder and wadding.

5

And you, Lady of Ships! you Mannahatta!
Old matron of this proud, friendly, turbulent city!
Often in peace and wealth you were pensive, or covertly
    frown'd amid all your children;
But now you smile with joy, exulting old Mannahatta!
                                                    1865

———————

EIGHTEEN SIXTY-ONE

*A*RM'D year! year of the struggle!
    No dainty rhymes or sentimental love verses for
        you, terrible year!
Not you as some pale poetling, seated at a desk, lisping
    cadenzas piano;
But as a strong man, erect, clothed in blue clothes, ad-
    vancing, carrying a rifle on your shoulder,
With well-gristled body and sunburnt face and hands—
    with a knife in the belt at your side,

As I heard you shouting loud—your sonorous voice ringing across the continent;
Your masculine voice, O year, as rising amid the great
  cities,
Amid the men of Manhattan I saw you, as one of the
  workmen, the dwellers in Manhattan;
Or with large steps crossing the prairies out of Illinois
  and Indiana,
Rapidly crossing the West with springy gait, and descend-
  ing the Alleghanies;
Or down from the great lakes, or in Pennsylvania, or on
  deck along the Ohio river;
Or southward along the Tennessee or Cumberland rivers,
  or at Chattanooga on the mountain top,
Saw I your gait and saw I your sinewy limbs, clothed in
  blue, bearing weapons, robust year;
Heard your determin'd voice, launch'd forth again and
  again;
Year that suddenly sang by the mouths of the round-
  lipp'd cannon,
I repeat you, hurrying, crashing, sad, distracted year. 1865

BEAT! BEAT! DRUMS!

1

*B*EAT! beat! drums!—Blow! bugles! blow!
  Through the windows—through doors—burst
    like a ruthless force,
Into the solemn church, and scatter the congregation;
Into the school where the scholar is studying;

[5]

Leave not the bridegroom quiet—no happiness must he
    have now with his bride;
Nor the peaceful farmer any peace, plowing his field or
    gathering his grain;
So fierce you whirr and pound, you drums—so shrill you
    bugles blow.

2

Beat! beat! drums!—Blow! bugles! blow!
Over the traffic of cities—over the rumble of wheels in
    the streets:
Are beds prepared for sleepers at night in the houses?
    No sleepers must sleep in those beds;
No bargainers' bargains by day—no brokers or specula-
    tors—Would they continue?
Would the talkers be talking? would the singer attempt
    to sing?
Would the lawyer rise in the court to state his case before
    the judge?
Then rattle quicker, heavier drums—you bugles, wilder
    blow.

3

Beat! beat! drums!—Blow! bugles! blow!
Make no parley—stop for no expostulation;
Mind not the timid—mind not the weeper or prayer;
Mind not the old man beseeching the young man;
Let not the child's voice be heard, nor the mother's en-
    treaties;
Make even the trestles to shake the dead, where they lie
    awaiting the hearses,
So strong you thump, O terrible drums—so loud you
    bugles blow.   1865

[6]

FROM PAUMANOK STARTING I FLY LIKE A BIRD

FROM Paumanok starting, I fly like a bird,
  Around and around to soar, to sing the idea of
    all;
To the north betaking myself, to sing their arctic songs,
To Kanada, till I absorb Kanada in myself—to Michigan
  then,
To Wisconsin, Iowa, Minnesota, to sing their songs, (they
  are inimitable;)
Then to Ohio and Indiana to sing theirs—to Missouri
  and Kansas and Arkansas, to sing theirs,
To Tennessee and Kentucky—to the Carolinas and
  Georgia, to sing theirs,
To Texas, and so along up toward California, to roam
  accepted everywhere;
To sing first, (to the tap of the war-drum, if need be,)
The idea of all—of the western world, one and insepa-
  rable.
And then the song of each member of These States. 1865

SONG OF THE BANNER AT DAY-BREAK

POET

O A NEW song, a free song,
  Flapping, flapping, flapping, flapping, by sounds,
    by voices clearer,
By the wind's voice and that of the drum,

DRUM TAPS . . . .

By the banner's voice, and child's voice, and sea's voice,
    and father's voice,
Low on the ground and high in the air,
On the ground where father and child stand,
In the upward air where their eyes turn,
Where the banner at day-break is flapping.

Words! book-words! what are you?
Words no more, for hearken and see,
My song is there in the open air—and I must sing,
With the banner and pennant a-flapping.
I'll weave the chord and twine in,
Man's desire and babe's desire—I'll twine them in, I'll
    put in life;
I'll put the bayonet's flashing point—I'll let bullets and
    slugs whizz;
(As one carrying a symbol and menace, far into the fu-
    ture,
Crying with trumpet voice, *Arouse and beware! Beware
    and arouse!*)
I'll pour the verse with streams of blood, full of volition,
    full of joy;
Then loosen, launch forth, to go and compete,
With the banner and pennant a-flapping.

PENNANT

Come up here, bard, bard;
Come up here, soul, soul;
Come up here, dear little child,
To fly in the clouds and winds with me, and play with the
    measureless light.

[8]

CHILD

Father, what is that in the sky beckoning to me with long
    finger?
And what does it say to me all the while?

FATHER

Nothing, my babe, you see in the sky;
And nothing at all to you it says. But look you, my babe,
Look at these dazzling things in the houses, and see you
    the money-shops opening;
And see you the vehicles preparing to crawl along the
    streets with goods:
These! ah, these! how valued and toil'd for, these!
How envied by all the earth!

POET

Fresh and rosy red, the sun is mounting high;
On floats the sea in distant blue, careering through its
    channels;
On floats the wind over the breast of the sea, setting in
    toward land;
The great steady wind from west and west-by-south,
Floating so buoyant, with milk-white foam on the waters.

But I am not the sea, nor the red sun;
I am not the wind, with girlish laughter;
Not the immense wind which strengthens—not the wind
    which lashes;
Not the spirit that ever lashes its own body to terror and
    death;

But I am that which unseen comes and sings, sings, sings,
Which babbles in brooks and scoots in showers on the
land,
Which the birds know in the woods, mornings and eve-
nings,
And the shore-sands know, and the hissing wave, and that
banner and pennant,
Aloft there flapping and flapping.

CHILD

O father, it is alive—it is full of people—it has children!
O now it seems to me it is talking to its children!
I hear it—it talks to me—O it is wonderful!
O it stretches—it spreads and runs so fast! O my father,
It is so broad, it covers the whole sky!

FATHER

Cease, cease, my foolish babe,
What you are saying is sorrowful to me—much it dis-
pleases me;
Behold with the rest, again I say—behold not banners
and pennants aloft;
But the well-prepared pavements behold—and mark the
solid wall'd houses.

BANNER AND PENNANT

Speak to the child, O bard, out of Manhattan;
(The war is over—yet never over . . . out of it, we are
born to real life and identity;)
Speak to our children all, or north or south of Manhattan,

Where our factory-engines hum, where our miners delve
    the ground,
Where our hoarse Niagara rumbles, where our prairie-
    plows are plowing;
Speak, O bard! point this day, leaving all the rest, to us
    over all—and yet we know not why;
For what are we, mere strips of cloth, profiting nothing,
Only flapping in the wind?

POET

I hear and see not strips of cloth alone;
I hear again the tramp of armies, I hear the challenging
    sentry;
I hear the jubilant shouts of millions of men—I hear
    LIBERTY!
I hear the drums beat, and the trumpets yet blowing;
I myself move abroad, swift-rising, flying then;
I use the wings of the land-bird, and use the wings of
    the sea-bird, and look down as from a height;
I do not deny the precious results of peace—I see popu-
    lous cities, with wealth incalculable;
I see numberless farms—I see the farmers working in
    their fields or barns;
I see mechanics working—I see buildings everywhere
    founded, going up, or finish'd;
I see trains of cars swiftly speeding along railroad tracks,
    drawn by the locomotives;
I see the stores, depots, of Boston, Baltimore, Charleston,
    New Orleans;
I see far in the west the immense area of grain—I dwell
    awhile, hovering;

[11]

I pass to the lumber forests of the north, and again to the
  southern plantation, and again to California;
Sweeping the whole, I see the countless profit, the busy
  gatherings, earned wages;
See the identity formed out of thirty-eight spacious and
  haughty States (and many more to come;)
See forts on the shores of harbors—see ships sailing in and
  out;
Then over all, (aye! aye!) my little and lengthen'd pennant, shaped like a sword,
Runs swiftly up, indicating war and defiance—and now
  the halyards have rais'd it,
Side of my banner broad and blue—side of my starry
  banner,
Discarding peace over all the sea and land.

Banner and Pennant

Yet louder, higher, stronger, bard! yet farther, wider
  cleave!
No longer let our children deem us riches and peace
  alone;
We may be terror and carnage, and are so now;
Not now are we any one of these spacious and haughty
  States, (nor any five, nor ten;)
Nor market nor depot are we, nor money-bank in the city;
But these, and all, and the brown and spreading land, and
  the mines below, are ours;
And the shores of the sea are ours, and the rivers, great
  and small;
And the fields they moisten are ours, and the crops and
  the fruits are ours;

Bays and channels, and ships sailing in and out, are ours—
and we over all,
Over the area spread below, the three or four millions of
square miles—the capitals,
The forty millions of people—O bard! in life and death
supreme,
We, even we, henceforth, flaunt out masterful, high up
above,
Not for the present alone, for a thousand years, chanting
through you,
This song to the soul of one poor little child.

CHILD

O my father, I like not the houses;
They will never to me be anything—nor do I like
money;
But to mount up there I would like, O father dear—that
banner I like;
That pennant I would be, and must be.

FATHER

Child of mine, you fill me with anguish;
To be that pennant would be too fearful;
Little you know what it is this day, and after this day,
forever;
It is to gain nothing, but risk and defy everything;
Forward to stand in front of wars—and O, such wars!—
what have you to do with them?
With passions of demons, slaughter, premature death?

Poet

Demons and death then I sing;

Put in all, aye, all, will I—sword-shaped pennant for war, and banner so broad and blue,

And a pleasure new and ecstatic, and the prattled yearning of children,

Blent with the sounds of the peaceful land, and the liquid wash of the sea;

And the black ships, fighting on the sea, enveloped in smoke;

And the icy cool of the far, far north, with rusting cedars and pines;

And the whirr of drums, and the sound of soldiers marching and the hot sun shining south;

And the beach-waves combing over the beach on my eastern shore, and my western shore the same;

And all between those shores, and my ever running Mississippi, with bends and chutes;

And my Illinois fields, and my Kansas fields, and my fields of Missouri;

The CONTINENT—devoting the whole identity, without reserving an atom,

Pour in! whelm that which asks, which sings, with all, and the yield of all.

Banner and Pennant

Aye all! for ever, for all!

From sea to sea, north and south, east and west,

(The war is completed, the price is paid, the title is settled beyond recall;)

Fusing and holding, claiming, devouring the whole;
No more with tender lip, nor musical labial sound,
But, out of the night emerging for good, our voice per-
    suasive no more,
Croaking like crows here in the wind.

POET
(*Finale*)

My limbs, my veins dilate;
The blood of the world has fill'd me full—my theme is
    clear at last:
—Banner so broad, advancing out of the night, I sing
    you haughty and resolute;
I burst through where I waited long, too long, deafen'd
    and blinded;
My sight, my hearing and tongue, are come to me, (a
    little child taught me;)
I hear from above, O pennant of war, your ironical call
    and demand;
Insensate! insensate! (yet I at any rate chant you,) O
    banner!
Not houses of peace indeed are you, nor any nor all their
    prosperity, (if need be, you shall again have every
    one of those houses to destroy them;
You thought not to destroy those valuable houses, stand-
    ing fast, full of comfort, built with money;
May they stand fast, then? Not an hour, except you, above
    them and all, stand fast;)
—O banner! not money so precious are you, not farm
    produce you, nor the material good nutriment,

Nor excellent stores, nor landed on wharves from the ships;

Not the superb ships, with sail-power or steam-power, fetching and carrying cargoes,

Nor machinery, vehicles, trade, nor revenues,—but you, as henceforth I see you,

Running up out of the night, bringing your cluster of stars, (ever-enlarging stars;)

Divider of day-break you, cutting the air, touch'd by the sun, measuring the sky,

(Passionately seen and yearn'd for by one poor little child,

While others remain busy, or smartly talking, forever teaching thrift, thrift;)

O you up there! O pennant! where you undulate like a snake, hissing so curious,

Out of reach—an idea only—yet furiously fought for, risking bloody death—loved by me!

So loved! O you banner leading the day, with stars brought from the night!

Valueless, object of eyes, over all and demanding all— (absolute owner of ALL)—O banner and pennant!

I too leave the rest—great as it is, it is nothing—houses, machines are nothing—I see them not;

I see but you, O warlike pennant! O banner so broad, with stripes, I sing you only,

Flapping up there in the wind.   1865

RISE, O DAYS, FROM YOUR FATHOMLESS DEEPS

1

RISE, O days, from your fathomless deeps, till you
   loftier, fiercer sweep!
   Long for my soul, hungering gymnastic, I de-
vour'd what the earth gave me;
Long I roam'd the woods of the north—long I watch'd
   Niagara pouring;
I travel'd the prairies over, and slept on their breast—I
   cross'd the Nevadas, I cross'd the plateaus;
I ascended the towering rocks along the Pacific, I sail'd
   out to sea;
I sail'd through the storm, I was refresh'd by the storm;
I watch'd with joy the threatening maws of the waves;
I mark'd the white combs where they career'd so high,
   curling over;
I heard the wind piping, I saw the black clouds;
Saw from below what arose and mounted, (O superb! O
   wild as my heart, and powerful!)
Heard the continuous thunder, as it bellow'd after the
   lightning;
Noted the slender and jagged threads of lightning, as sud-
   den and fast amid the din they chased each other
   across the sky;
—These, and such as these, I, elate, saw—saw with won-
   der, yet pensive and masterful;
All the menacing might of the globe uprisen around me;
Yet there with my soul I fed—I fed content, supercilious.

[17]

2

'Twas well, O soul! 'twas a good preparation you gave me!

Now we advance our latent and ampler hunger to fill;

Now we go forth to receive what the earth and the sea
never gave us;

Not through the mighty woods we go, but through the
mightier cities;

Something for us is pouring now, more than Niagara
pouring;

Torrents of men, (sources and rills of the Northwest,
are you indeed inexhaustible?)

What, to pavements and homesteads here—what were
those storms of the mountains and sea?

What, to passions I witness around me to-day? Was the sea
risen?

Was the wind piping the pipe of death under the black
clouds?

Lo! from deeps more unfathomable, something more
deadly and savage;

Manhattan, rising, advancing with menacing front—Cin-
cinnati, Chicago, unchain'd;

—What was that swell I saw on the ocean? behold what
comes here!

How it climbs with daring feet and hands! how it dashes!

How the true thunder bellows after the lightning! how
bright the flashes of lightning!

How DEMOCRACY, with desperate vengeful port strides on,
shown through the dark by those flashes of lightning!

(Yet a mournful wail and low sob I fancied I heard
through the dark,

In a lull of deafening confusion.)

3

Thunder on! stride on, Democracy! strike with vengeful
    stroke!
And do you rise higher than ever yet, O days, O cities!
Crash heavier, heavier. yet, O storms! you have done me
    good;
My soul, prepared in the mountains, absorbs your im-
    mortal strong nutriment;
Long had I walk'd my cities, my country roads, through
    farms, only half-satisfied;
One doubt, nauseous, undulating like a snake, crawl'd on
    the ground before me,
Continually preceding my steps, turning upon me oft,
    ironically hissing low;
—The cities I loved so well, I abandon'd and left—I sped
    to the certainties suitable to me;
Hungering, hungering, hungering, for primal energies,
    and Nature's dauntlessness,
I refresh'd myself with it only, I could relish it only;
I waited the bursting forth of the pent fire—on the water
    and air I waited long;
—But now I no longer wait—I am fully satisfied—I am
    glutted;
I have witness'd the true lightning—I have witness'd my
    cities electric;
I have lived to behold man burst forth, and warlike
    America rise;
Hence I will seek no more the food of the northern
    solitary wilds,
No more on the mountains roam, or sail the stormy sea.

1865

[19]

CITY OF SHIPS

CITY of ships!
　　(O the black ships! O the fierce ships!
　　O the beautiful, sharp-bow'd steam-ships and sail-
　　　　ships!)
City of the world! (for all races are here;
All the lands of the earth make contributions here;)
City of the sea! city of hurried and glittering tides!
City whose gleeful tides continually rush or recede,
　　whirling in and out, with eddies and foam!
City of wharves and stores! city of tall façades of marble
　　and iron!
Proud and passionate city! mettlesome, mad, extravagant
　　city!
Spring up, O city! not for peace alone, but be indeed
　　yourself, warlike!
Fear not! submit to no models but your own, O city!
Behold me! incarnate me, as I have incarnated you!
I have rejected nothing you offer'd me—whom you
　　adopted, I have adopted;
Good or bad, I never question you—I love all—I do not
　　condemn anything;
I chant and celebrate all that is yours—yet peace no more;
In peace I chanted peace, but now the drum of war is
　　mine;
War, red war, is my song through your streets, O city!

1865

[20]

CAVALRY CROSSING A FORD

A LINE in long array, where they wind betwixt
         green islands;
      They take a serpentine course—their arms flash
         in the sun—hark to the musical clank;
Behold the silvery river—in it the splashing horses,
      loitering, stop to drink;
Behold the brown-faced men—each group, each person,
      a picture—the negligent rest on the saddles;
Some emerge on the opposite bank—others are just enter-
      ing the ford—while,
Scarlet, and blue, and snowy white,
The guidon flags flutter gaily in the wind.   1865

BIVOUAC ON A MOUNTAIN SIDE

I SEE before me now, a traveling army halting;
      Below, a fertile valley spread, with barns, and the
         orchards of summer;
Behind, the terraced sides of a mountain, abrupt in places,
      rising high;
Broken, with rocks, with clinging cedars, with tall shapes,
      dingily seen;
The numerous camp-fires scatter'd near and far, some
      away up on the mountain;
The shadowy forms of men and horses, looming, large-
      sized, flickering;
And over all, the sky—the sky! far, far out of reach,
      studded, breaking out, the eternal stars.   1865

[21]

AN ARMY CORPS ON THE MARCH

*W*ITH its cloud of skirmishers in advance,
With now the sound of a single shot, snapping
like a whip, and now an irregular volley,
The swarming ranks press on and on, the dense brigades
press on;
Glittering dimly, toiling under the sun—the dust-cover'd
men,
In columns rise and fall to the undulations of the ground,
With artillery interspers'd—the wheels rumble, the horses
sweat,
As the army corps advances.   1865

BY THE BIVOUAC'S FITFUL FLAME

*B*Y the bivouac's fitful flame,
A procession winding around me, solemn and
sweet and slow;—but first I note,
The tents of the sleeping army, the fields' and woods' dim
outline,
The darkness, lit by spots of kindled fire—the silence;
Like a phantom far or near an occasional figure moving;
The shrubs and trees, (as I lift my eyes they seem to be
stealthily watching me;)
While wind in procession thoughts, O tender and won-
drous thoughts,
Of life and death—of home and the past and loved, and
of those that are far away;
A solemn and slow procession there as I sit on the ground,
By the bivouac's fitful flame.   1865

COME UP FROM THE FIELDS, FATHER

1

*C*OME up from the fields, father, here's a letter
from our Pete;
And come to the front door, mother—here's a
letter from thy dear son.

2

Lo, 'tis autumn;
Lo, where the trees, deeper green, yellower and redder,
Cool and sweeten Ohio's villages, with leaves fluttering in
the moderate wind;
Where apples ripe in the orchards hang, and grapes on
the trellis'd vines;
(Smell you the smell of the grapes on the vines?
Smell you the buckwheat, where the bees were lately
buzzing?)
Above all, lo, the sky, so calm, so transparent after the
rain, and with wondrous clouds;
Below, too, all calm, all vital and beautiful—and the
farm prospers well.

3

Down in the fields all prospers well;
But now from the fields come, father—come at the daughter's call;
And come to the entry, mother—to the front door come,
right away.

Fast as she can she hurries—something ominous—her
   steps trembling;
She does not tarry to smooth her hair, nor adjust her cap.

Open the envelope quickly;
O this is not our son's writing, yet his name is sign'd;
O a strange hand writes for our dear son—O stricken
   mother's soul!
All swims before her eyes—flashes with black—she catches
   the main words only;
Sentences broken—*gun-shot wound in the breast, cavalry
   skirmish, taken to hospital,*
At present low, but will soon be better.

4

Ah, now, the single figure to me,
Amid all teeming and wealthy Ohio, with all its cities and
   farms,
Sickly white in the face, and dull in the head, very faint,
By the jamb of a door leans.

Grieve not so, dear mother, (the just-grown daughter
   speaks through her sobs;
The little sisters huddle around, speechless and dismay'd;)
*See, dearest mother, the letter says Pete will soon be
   better.*

5

Alas, poor boy, he will never be better, (nor may-be needs
   to be better, that brave and simple soul;)
While they stand at home at the door, he is dead already;
The only son is dead.

But the mother needs to be better;
She, with thin form, presently drest in black;
By day her meals untouch'd—then at night fitfully sleep-
    ing, often waking,
In the midnight waking, weeping, longing with one deep
    longing,
O that she might withdraw unnoticed—silent from life,
    escape and withdraw,
To follow, to seek, to be with her dear dead son.   1865.

VIGIL STRANGE I KEPT ON THE FIELD
ONE NIGHT

VIGIL strange I kept on the field one night:
    When you, my son and my comrade, dropt at my
        side that day,
One look I but gave, which your dear eyes return'd, with
    a look I shall never forget;
One touch of your hand to mine, O boy, reach'd up as
    you lay on the ground;
Then onward I sped in the battle, the even-contested
    battle;
Till late in the night reliev'd, to the place at last again I
    made my way;
Found you in death so cold, dear comrade—found your
    body, son of responding kisses, (never again on earth
    responding;)
Bared your face in the starlight—curious the scene—cool
    blew the moderate night-wind;

DRUM TAPS . . . .

Long there and then in vigil I stood, dimly around me
the battle-field spreading;
Vigil wondrous and vigil sweet, there in the fragrant
silent night;
But not a tear fell, not even a long-drawn sigh—long, long
I gazed;
Then on the earth partially reclining, sat by your side,
leaning my chin in my hands;
Passing sweet hours, immortal and mystic hours with you,
dearest comrade—not a tear, not a word;
Vigil of silence, love and death—vigil for you, my son
and my soldier,
As onward silently stars aloft, eastward new ones upward
stole;
Vigil final for you, brave boy, (I could not save you,
swift was your death,
I faithfully loved you and cared for you living—I think
we shall surely meet again;)
Till at latest lingering of the night, indeed just as the
dawn appear'd,
My comrade I wrapt in his blanket, envelop'd well his
form,
Folded the blanket well, tucking it carefully over head,
and carefully under feet;
And there and then, and bathed by the rising sun, my
son in his grave, in his rude-dug grave I deposited;
Ending my vigil strange with that—vigil of night and
battlefield dim;
Vigil for boy of responding kisses, (never again on earth
responding;)

Vigil for comrade swiftly slain—vigil I never forget, how
as day brighten'd,
I rose from the chill ground, and folded my soldier well
in his blanket,
And buried him where he fell.   1865

A MARCH IN THE RANKS HARD-PREST, AND THE ROAD UNKNOWN

A MARCH in the ranks hard-prest, and the road
unknown;
A route through a heavy wood, with muffled
steps in the darkness;
Our army foil'd with loss severe, and the sullen remnant
retreating;
Till after midnight glimmer upon us, the lights of a dim-
lighted building;
We come to an open space in the woods, and halt by the
dim-lighted building;
'Tis a large old church at the crossing roads—'tis now an
impromptu hospital;
—Entering but for a minute, I see a sight beyond all the
pictures and poems ever made:
Shadows of deepest, deepest black, just lit by moving
candles and lamps,
And by one great pitchy torch, stationary, with wild red
flame, and clouds of smoke;
By these crowds, groups of forms, vaguely I see, on the
floor, some in the pews laid down;

DRUM TAPS . . . .

At my feet more distinctly, a soldier, a mere lad, in
    danger of bleeding to death, (he is shot in the
    abdomen;)
I staunch the blood temporarily, (the youngster's face is
    white as a lily;)
Then before I depart I sweep my eyes o'er the scene, fain
    to absorb it all;
Faces, varieties, postures beyond description, most in ob-
    scurity, some of them dead;
Surgeons operating, attendants holding lights, the smell
    of ether, the odor of blood;
The crowd, O the crowd of the bloody forms of soldiers—
    the yard outside also fill'd;
Some on the bare ground, some on planks or stretchers,
    some in the death-spasm sweating;
An occasional scream or cry, the doctor's shouted orders
    or calls;
The glisten of the little steel instruments catching the
    glint of the torches;
These I resume as I chant—I see again the forms, I smell
    the odor;
Then hear outside the orders given, *Fall in, my men,
    fall in;*
But first I bend to the dying lad—his eyes open—a half-
    smile gives he me;
Then the eyes close, calmly close, and I speed forth to
    the darkness,
Resuming, marching, ever in darkness marching, on in
    the ranks,
The unknown road still marching.   1865

[28]

A SIGHT IN CAMP IN THE DAY-BREAK GRAY
AND DIM

A SIGHT in camp in the day-break gray and dim,
As from my tent I emerge so early, sleepless,
As slow I walk in the cool fresh air, the path near
 by the hospital tent,
Three forms I see on stretchers lying, brought out there,
 untended lying,
Over each the blanket spread, ample brownish woollen
 blanket,
Gray and heavy blanket, folding, covering all.

Curious, I halt, and silent stand;
Then with light fingers I from the face of the nearest,
 the first, just lift the blanket:
Who are you, elderly man so gaunt and grim, with well-
 gray'd hair, and flesh all sunken about the eyes?
Who are you, my dear comrade?

Then to the second I step—and who are you, my child
 and darling?
Who are you, sweet boy, with cheeks yet blooming?

Then to the third—a face nor child, nor old, very calm,
 as of beautiful yellow-white ivory;
Young man, I think I know you—I think this face of
 yours is the face of Christ himself;
Dead and divine, and brother of all, and here again he
 lies.   1865

[29]

AS TOILSOME I WANDER'D VIRGINIA'S WOODS

AS TOILSOME I wander'd Virginia's woods,
    To the music of rustling leaves, kick'd by my
      feet, (for 'twas autumn,)
I mark'd at the foot of a tree the grave of a soldier,
Mortally wounded he, and buried on the retreat, (easily
    all could I understand;)
The halt of a mid-day hour, when up! no time to lose—
    yet this sign left,
On a tablet scrawl'd and nail'd on the tree by the grave,
Bold, cautious, true, and my loving comrade.

Long, long I muse, then on my way go wandering;
Many a changeful season to follow, and many a scene of
    life;
Yet at times through changeful season and scene, abrupt,
    alone, or in the crowded street,
Comes before me the unknown soldier's grave—comes the
    inscription rude in Virginia's woods,
Bold, cautious, true, and my loving comrade.   1865

YEAR THAT TREMBLED AND REEL'D BENEATH ME

YEAR that trembled and reel'd beneath me!
    Your summer wind was warm enough—yet the
      air I breathed froze me;
A thick gloom fell through the sunshine and darken'd
    me;

[30]

Must I change my triumphant songs? said I to myself;
Must I indeed learn to chant the cold dirges of the
baffled?
And sullen hymns of defeat?   1865

THE DRESSER

1

*A*N old man bending, I come, among new faces,
      Years looking backward, resuming, in answer to
         children,
Come tell us, old man, as from young men and maidens
   that love me;
Years hence of these scenes, of these furious passions,
   these chances,
Of unsurpass'd heroes, (was one side so brave? the other
   was equally brave;)
Now be witness again—paint the mightiest armies of
   earth;
Of those armies so rapid, so wondrous, what saw you to
   tell us?
What stays with you latest and deepest? of curious panics,
Of hard-fought engagements, or sieges tremendous, what
   deepest remains?

2

O maidens and young men I love, and that love me,
What you ask of my days, those the strangest and sudden
   your talking recalls;
Soldier alert I arrive, after a long march, cover'd with
   sweat and dust;

DRUM TAPS . . . .

In the nick of time I come, plunge in the fight, loudly
    shout in the rush of successful charge;
Enter the captur'd works . . . yet lo! like a swift-run-
    ning river, they fade;
Pass and are gone, they fade—I dwell not on soldiers'
    perils or soldiers' joys;
(Both I remember well—many the hardships, few the
    joys, yet I was content.)

But in silence, in dreams' projections,
While the world of gain and appearance and mirth goes
    on,
So soon what is over forgotten, and waves wash the im-
    prints off the sand,
In nature's reveries sad, with hinged knees returning, I
    enter the doors— (while for you up there,
Whoever you are, follow me without noise, and be of
    strong heart.)

3

Bearing the bandages, water and sponge,
Straight and swift to my wounded I go,
Where they lie on the ground, after the battle brought in;
Where their priceless blood reddens the grass, the ground;
Or to the rows of the hospital tent, or under the roof'd
    hospital;
To the long rows of cots, up and down, each side, I re-
    turn;
To each and all, one after another, I draw near—not one
    do I miss;

An attendant follows, holding a tray—he carries a refuse
  pail,
Soon to be fill'd with clotted rags and blood, emptied and
  fill'd again.

I onward go, I stop,
With hinged knees and steady hand, to dress wounds;
I am firm with each—the pangs are sharp, yet unavoid-
  able;
One turns to me his appealing eyes—(poor boy! I never
  knew you,
Yet I think I could not refuse this moment to die for
  you, if that would save you.)

4

On, on I go!—(open doors of time! open hospital doors!)
The crush'd head I dress, (poor crazed hand, tear not the
  bandage away;)
The neck of the cavalry-man, with the bullet through and
  through, I examine;
Hard the breathing rattles, quite glazed already the eye,
  yet life struggles hard;
(Come, sweet death! be persuaded, O beautiful death!
In mercy come quickly.)

From the stump of the arm, the amputated hand,
I undo the clotted lint, remove the slough, wash off the
  matter and blood;
Back on his pillow the soldier bends, with curv'd neck,
  and side-falling head;

His eyes are closed, his face is pale, (he dares not look on
the bloody stump,
And has not yet look'd on it.)

I dress a wound in the side, deep, deep;
But a day or two more—for see, the frame all wasted
already, and sinking,
And the yellow-blue countenance see.
I dress the perforated shoulder, the foot with the bullet
wound,
Cleanse the one with a gnawing and putrid gangrene, so
sickening, so offensive,
While the attendant stands behind aside me, holding the
tray and pail.

I am faithful, I do not give out;
The fractur'd thigh, the knee, the wound in the abdomen,
These and more I dress with impassive hand— (yet deep
in my breast a fire, a burning flame.)

5

Thus in silence, in dreams' projections,
Returning, resuming, I thread my way through the hos-
pitals;
The hurt and wounded I pacify with soothing hand,
I sit by the restless all the dark night—some are so young;
Some suffer so much—I recall the experience sweet and
sad;
(Many a soldier's loving arms about this neck have
cross'd and rested,
Many a soldier's kiss dwells on these bearded lips.)

1865

[34]

LONG, TOO LONG, O LAND

LONG, too long, O land,
   Traveling roads all even and peaceful, you
      learn'd from joys and prosperity only;
But now, ah now, to learn from crises of anguish—advancing, grappling with direst fate, and recoiling not;
And now to conceive, and show to the world, what your
   children en-masse really are;
(For who except myself has yet conceiv'd what your children en-masse really are?)   1865

GIVE ME THE SPLENDID SILENT SUN

1

GIVE me the splendid silent sun, with all his beams
      full-dazzling;
   Give me juicy autumnal fruit, ripe and red from
      the orchard;
Give me a field where the unmow'd grass grows,
Give me an arbor, give me the trellis'd grape;
Give me fresh corn and wheat—give me serene-moving
   animals, teaching content;
Give me nights perfectly quiet, as on high plateaus west
   of the Mississippi, and I looking up at the stars;
Give me odorous at sunrise a garden of beautiful flowers,
   where I can walk undisturb'd;
Give me for marriage a sweet-breath'd woman, of whom
   I should never tire;

[35]

Give me a perfect child—give me, away, aside from the
noise of the world, a rural, domestic life;
Give me to warble spontaneous songs, reliev'd, recluse by
myself, for my own ears only;
Give me solitude—give me Nature—give me again, O
Nature, your primal sanities!
—These, demanding to have them, (tired with ceaseless
excitement, and rack'd by the war-strife;)
These to procure, incessantly asking, rising in cries from
my heart,
While yet incessantly asking, still I adhere to my city;
Day upon day, and year upon year, O city, walking your
streets,
Where you hold me enchain'd a certain time, refusing to
give me up;
Yet giving to make me glutted, enrich'd of soul—you give
me forever faces;
(O I see what I sought to escape, confronting, reversing
my cries;
I see my own soul trampling down what it ask'd for.)

2

Keep your splendid, silent sun;
Keep your woods, O Nature, and the quiet places by the
woods;
Keep your fields of clover and timothy, and your corn-
fields and orchards;
Keep the blossoming buckwheat fields, where the Ninth-
month bees hum;
Give me faces and streets! give me these phantoms incessant and endless along the trottoirs!

Give me interminable eyes! give me women! give me com-
    rades and lovers by the thousand!
Let me see new ones every day! let me hold new ones by
    the hand every day!
Give me such shows! give me the streets of Manhattan!
Give me Broadway, with the soldiers marching—give me
    the sound of the trumpets and drums!
(The soldiers in companies or regiments—some, starting
    away, flush'd and reckless;
Some, their time up, returning, with thinn'd ranks—
    young, yet very old, worn, marching, noticing noth-
    ing;)
—Give me the shores and the wharves heavy-fringed with
    the black ships!
O such for me! O an intense life! O full to repletion, and
    varied!
The life of the theater, bar-room, huge hotel, for me!
The saloon of the steamer! the crowded excursion for me!
    the torch-light procession!
The dense brigade, bound for the war, with high piled
    military wagons following;
People, endless, streaming, with strong voices, passions,
    pageants;
Manhattan streets, with their powerful throbs, with the
    beating drums, as now;
The endless and noisy chorus, the rustle and clank of
    muskets, (even the sight of the wounded;)
Manhattan crowds, with their turbulent musical chorus—
    with varied chorus, and light of the sparkling eyes;
Manhattan faces and eyes forever for me.   1865

DIRGE FOR TWO VETERANS

1

THE last sunbeam
Lightly falls from the finish'd Sabbath,
On the pavement here—and there beyond, it is looking,
Down a new-made double grave.

2

Lo! the moon ascending!
Up from the east, the silvery round moon;
Beautiful over the house tops, ghastly phantom moon;
Immense and silent moon.

3

I see a sad procession,
And I hear the sound of coming full-key'd bugles;
All the channels of the city streets they're flooding,
As with voices and with tears.

4

I hear the great drums pounding,
And the small drums steady whirring;
And every blow of the great convulsive drums,
Strikes me through and through.

5

For the son is brought with the father;
In the foremost ranks of the fierce assault they fell;
Two veterans, son and father, dropt together,
And the double grave awaits them.

6

Now nearer blow the bugles,
And the drums strike more convulsive;
And the day-light o'er the pavement quite has faded,
    And the strong dead-march enwraps me.

7

In the eastern sky up-buoying,
The sorrowful vast phantom moves illumin'd;
('Tis some mother's large, transparent face,
    In heaven brighter growing.)

8

O strong dead-march, you please me!
O moon immense, with your silvery face you soothe me!
O my soldiers twain! O my veterans, passing to burial!
    What I have I also give you.

9

The moon gives you light,
And the bugles and the drums give you music;
And my heart, O my soldiers, my veterans,
    My heart gives you love.   1865

OVER THE CARNAGE ROSE PROPHETIC A VOICE

OVER the carnage rose prophetic a voice,
    Be not dishearten'd—Affection shall solve the
        problems of Freedom yet;
Those who love each other shall become invincible—
    they shall yet make Columbia victorious.

Sons of the Mother of All! you shall yet be victorious!
You shall yet laugh to scorn the attacks of all the re-
    mainder of the earth.

No danger shall balk Columbia's lovers;
If need be, a thousand shall sternly immolate themselves
    for one.

One from Massachusetts shall be a Missourian's comrade;
From Maine and from hot Carolina, and another, an
    Oregonese, shall be friends triune,
More precious to each other than all the riches of the
    earth.

To Michigan, Florida perfumes shall tenderly come;
Not the perfumes of flowers, but sweeter, and wafted be-
    yond death.

It shall be customary in the houses and streets to see
    manly affection;
The most dauntless and rude shall touch face to face
    lightly;
The dependence of Liberty shall be lovers,
The continuance of Equality shall be comrades.

These shall tie you and band you stronger than hoops of
    iron;
I, ecstatic, O partners! O lands! with the love of lovers tie
    you.

(Were you looking to be held together by the lawyers?
Or by an agreement on a paper? or by arms?
—Nay—nor the world, nor any living thing, will so
    cohere.)   1865

I SAW OLD GENERAL AT BAY

I SAW old General at bay;
　　(Old as he was, his gray eyes yet shone out in
　　　battle like stars;)
His small force was now completely hemm'd in, in his
　works;
He call'd for volunteers to run the enemy's lines—a
　desperate emergency;
I saw a hundred and more step forth from the ranks—but
　two or three were selected;
I saw them receive their orders aside—they listen'd with
　care—the adjutant was very grave;
I saw them depart with cheerfulness, freely risking their
　lives.　　　　　　　　　　　　　　　　　1865

THE ARTILLERYMAN'S VISION

*W*HILE my wife at my side lies slumbering, and
　　the wars are over long,
　　And my head on the pillow rests at home, and
　　　the vacant midnight passes,
And through the stillness, through the dark, I hear, just
　hear, the breath of my infant,
There in the room, as I wake from sleep, this vision
　presses upon me:
The engagement opens there and then, in fantasy unreal;
The skirmishers begin—they crawl cautiously ahead—I
　hear the irregular snap! snap!

DRUM TAPS . . . .

I hear the sound of the different missiles—the short *t-h-t!*
    t-h-t! of the rifle balls;
I see the shells exploding, leaving small white clouds—I
    hear the great shells shrieking as they pass;
The grape, like the hum and whirr of wind through the
    trees, (quick, tumultuous, now the contest rages!)
All the scenes at the batteries themselves rise in detail
    before me again;
The crashing and smoking—the pride of the men in their
    pieces;
The chief gunner ranges and sights his piece, and selects
    a fuse of the right time;
After firing, I see him lean aside, and look eagerly off to
    note the effect;
—Elsewhere I hear the cry of a regiment charging— (the
    young colonel leads himself this time, with brandish'd
    sword;)
I see the gaps cut by the enemy's volleys, (quickly fill'd
    up, no delay;)
I breathe the suffocating smoke—then the flat clouds
    hover low, concealing all;
Now a strange lull comes for a few seconds, not a shot
    fired on either side;
Then resumed, the chaos louder than ever, with eager
    calls, and orders of officers;
While from some distant part of the field the wind wafts
    to my ears a shout of applause, (some special suc-
    cess;)
And ever the sound of the cannon, far or near, (rousing,
    even in dreams, a devilish exultation, and all the old
    mad joy, in the depths of my soul;)

And ever the hastening of infantry shifting positions—
    batteries, cavalry, moving hither and thither;
(The falling, dying, I heed not—the wounded, dripping
    and red, I heed not—some to the rear are hobbling;)
Grime, heat, rush—aides-de-camp galloping by, or on a
    full run;
With the patter of small arms, the warning *s-s-t* of the
    rifles, (these in my vision I hear or see,)
And bombs bursting in air, and at night the vari-color'd
    rockets.   1865

NOT YOUTH PERTAINS TO ME

*N*OT youth pertains to me,
    Nor delicatesse—I cannot beguile the time with
    talk;
Awkward in the parlor, neither a dancer nor elegant;
In the learn'd coterie sitting constrain'd and still—for
    learning inures not to me;
Beauty, knowledge, inure not to me—yet there are two
    or three things inure to me;
I have nourish'd the wounded, and sooth'd many a dying
    soldier,
And at intervals, waiting, or in the midst of camp,
Composed these songs.   1865

DRUM TAPS . . . .

RACE OF VETERANS

RACE of veterans! Race of victors!
Race of the soil, ready for conflict! race of the
conquering march!
(No more credulity's race, abiding-temper'd race;)
Race henceforth owning no law but the law of itself;
Race of passion and the storm.   1865

WORLD, TAKE GOOD NOTICE

WORLD, take good notice, silver stars fading,
Milky hue ript, weft of white detaching,
Coals thirty-eight, baleful and burning,
Scarlet, significant, hands off warning,
Now and henceforth flaunt from these shores.   1865

O TAN-FACED PRAIRIE-BOY

O TAN-FACED prairie-boy!
Before you came to camp, came many a welcome
gift;
Praises and presents came, and nourishing food—till at
last, among the recruits,
You came, taciturn, with nothing to give—we but look'd
on each other,
When lo! more than all the gifts of the world, you gave
me.   1865

[44]

LOOK DOWN, FAIR MOON

*L*OOK down, fair moon, and bathe this scene;
   Pour softly down night's nimbus floods, on faces
      ghastly, swollen, purple;
On the dead, on their backs, with their arms toss'd wide,
Pour down your unstinted nimbus, sacred moon.   1865

RECONCILIATION

*W*ORD over all, beautiful as the sky!
   Beautiful that war, and all its deeds of carnage,
      must in time be utterly lost;
That the hands of the sisters Death and Night, inces-
   santly softly wash again, and ever again, this soil'd
   world;
. . . For my enemy is dead—a man divine as myself is dead;
I look where he lies, white-faced and still, in the coffin—I
   draw near;
I bend down, and touch lightly with my lips the white
   face in the coffin.   1865

HOW SOLEMN AS ONE BY ONE

(WASHINGTON CITY, 1865)

*H*OW solemn, as one by one,
   As the ranks returning, all worn and sweaty—
      as the men file by where I stand;
As the faces, the masks appear—as I glance at the faces,
   studying the masks;

(As I glance upward out of this page, studying you, dear
    friend, whoever you are;)
How solemn the thought of my whispering soul, to each
    in the ranks, and to you;
I see behind each mask, that wonder, a kindred soul;
O the bullet could never kill what you really are, dear
    friend,
Nor the bayonet stab what you really are:
. . . The soul! yourself, I see, great as any, good as the
    best,
Waiting, secure and content, which the bullet could never
    kill,
Nor the bayonet stab, O friend!   1865

AS I LAY WITH MY HEAD IN YOUR LAP, CAMERADO

AS I lay with my head in your lap, Camerado,
    The confession I made I resume—what I said
    to you in the open air I resume:
I know I am restless, and make others so;
I know my words are weapons, full of danger, full of
    death;
(Indeed I am myself the real soldier;
It is not he, there, with his bayonet, and not the red-
    striped artilleryman;)
For I confront peace, security, and all the settled laws, to
    unsettle them;
I am more resolute because all have denied me, than I
    could ever have been had all accepted me;

[46]

I heed not, and have never heeded, either experience,
 caution, majorities, nor ridicule;
And the threat of what is call'd hell is little or nothing
 to me;
And the lure of what is call'd heaven is little or nothing
 to me;
. . . Dear Camerado! I confess I have urged you onward
 with me, and still urge you, without the least idea
 what is our destination,
Or whether we shall be victorious, or utterly quell'd and
 defeated.   1865

TO A CERTAIN CIVILIAN

ID you ask dulcet rhymes from me?
 Did you seek the civilian's peaceful and lan-
 guishing rhymes?
Did you find what I sang erewhile so hard to follow?
Why, I was not singing erewhile for you to follow, to
 understand—nor am I now;
(I have been born of the same as the war was born;
The drum-corps' harsh rattle is to me sweet music—I love
 well the martial dirge,
With slow wail, and convulsive throb, leading the officer's
 funeral:)
—What to such as you, anyhow, such a poet as I?—there-
 fore leave my works,
And go lull yourself with what you can understand—and
 with piano-tunes;
For I lull nobody—and you will never understand me.
                                                              1865

LO! VICTRESS ON THE PEAKS!

*L*O! Victress on the peaks!
　　　Where thou, with mighty brow, regarding the
　　　world,
(The world, O Libertad, that vainly conspired against
　　thee;)
Out of its countless beleaguering toils, after thwarting
　　them all;
Dominant, with the dazzling sun around thee,
Flauntest now unharm'd, in immortal soundness and
　　bloom—lo! in these hours supreme,
No poem proud, I, chanting, bring to thee—nor mastery's
　　rapturous verse;
But a book, containing night's darkness, and blood-drip-
　　ping wounds,
And psalms of the dead.　　　　　　　　　　　　1865

———

SPIRIT WHOSE WORK IS DONE

(WASHINGTON CITY, 1865)

*S*PIRIT whose work is done! spirit of dreadful
　　　hours!
　　　Ere, departing, fade from my eyes your forests
　　　of bayonets;
Spirit of gloomiest fears and doubts, (yet onward ever
　　unfaltering pressing;)
Spirit of many a solemn day, and many a savage scene!
　　electric spirit!

That with muttering voice, through the war now closed,
    like a tireless phantom flitted,
Rousing the land with breath of flame, while you beat
    and beat the drum;
—Now, as the sound of the drum, hollow and harsh to
    the last, reverberates round me;
As your ranks, your immortal ranks, return, return from
    the battles;
While the muskets of the young men yet lean over their
    shoulders;
While I look on the bayonets bristling over their
    shoulders;
While those slanted bayonets, whole forests of them,
    appearing in the distance, approach and pass on, re-
    turning homeward,
Moving with steady motion, swaying to and fro, to the
    right and left,
Evenly, lightly rising and falling, as the steps keep time;
—Spirit of hours I knew, all hectic red one day, but pale
    as death next day;
Touch my mouth, ere you depart—press my lips close!
Leave me your pulses of rage! bequeath them to me! fill
    me with currents convulsive!
Let them scorch and blister out of my chants, when you
    are gone;
Let them identify you to the future, in these songs.   1865

TURN, O LIBERTAD

TURN, O Libertad, for the war is over,
    (From it and all henceforth expanding, doubt-
       ing no more, resolute, sweeping the world,)
Turn from lands, retrospective, recording proofs of the
    past;
From the singers that sing the trailing glories of the past;
From the chants of the feudal world—the triumphs of
    kings, slavery, caste;
Turn to the world, the triumphs reserv'd and to come—
    give up that backward world;
Leave to the singers of hitherto—give them the trailing
    past;
But what remains, remains for singers for you—wars to
    come are for you;
(Lo! how the wars of the past have duly inured to you—
    and the wars of the present also inure:)
—Then turn, and be not alarm'd, O Libertad—turn your
    undying face,
To where the future, greater than all the past,
Is swiftly, surely preparing for you.   1865

TO THE LEAVEN'D SOIL THEY TROD

TO the leaven'd soil they trod, calling, I sing, for
    the last;
    (Not cities, nor man alone, nor war, nor the dead,
But forth from my tent emerging for good—loosing, un-
    tying the tent-ropes;)

[50]

In the freshness, the forenoon air, in the far-stretching
    circuits and vistas, again to peace restored,
To the fiery fields emanative, and the endless vistas be-
    yond—to the south and the north;
To the leaven'd soil of the general western world, to
    attest my songs,
(To the average earth, the wordless earth, witness of war
    and peace,)
To the Alleghanian hills, and the tireless Mississippi,
To the rocks I, calling, sing, and all the trees in the woods,
To the plain of the poems of heroes, to the prairie spread-
    ing wide,
To the far-off sea, and the unseen winds, and the same
    impalpable air;
. . . And responding, they answer all, (but not in words,)
The average earth, the witness of war and peace, acknowl-
    edges mutely;
The prairie draws me close, as the father, to bosom broad,
    the son;
The Northern ice and rain, that began me, nourish me
    to the end;
But the hot sun of the South is to ripen my songs.   1865

———

WHEN LILACS LAST IN THE DOOR-YARD
BLOOM'D

1

WHEN lilacs last in the door-yard bloom'd,
    And the great star early droop'd in the west-
    ern sky in the night,
I mourn'd—and yet shall mourn with ever-returning spring.

O ever-returning spring! trinity sure to me you bring;
Lilac blooming perennial, and drooping star in the west,
And thought of him I love.

2

O powerful, western, fallen star!
O shades of night! O moody, tearful night!
O great star disappear'd! O the black murk that hides
    the star!
O cruel hands that hold me powerless! O helpless soul of
    me!
O harsh surrounding cloud, that will not free my soul!

3

In the door-yard fronting an old farm-house, near the
    whitewash'd palings,
Stands the lilac bush, tall-growing, with heart-shaped
    leaves of rich green,
With many a pointed blossom, rising, delicate, with the
    perfume strong I love,
With every leaf a miracle . . . and from this bush in the
    door-yard,
With delicate-color'd blossoms, and heart-shaped leaves of
    rich green,
A sprig, with its flower, I break.

4

In the swamp, in secluded recesses,
A shy and hidden bird is warbling a song.
Solitary, the thrush,
The hermit, withdrawn to himself, avoiding the settle-
    ments,

Sings by himself a song.
Song of the bleeding throat!
Death's outlet song of life— (for well, dear brother, I know
If thou wast not gifted to sing, thou would'st surely die.)

5

Over the breast of the spring, the land, amid cities,
Amid lanes, and through old woods, (where lately the
    violets peep'd from the ground, spotting the gray
    debris;)
Amid the grass in the fields each side of the lanes—passing
    the endless grass;
Passing the yellow-spear'd wheat, every grain from its
    shroud in the dark-brown fields uprising;
Passing the apple-tree blows of white and pink in the or-
    chards;
Carrying a corpse to where it shall rest in the grave,
Night and day journeys a coffin.

6

Coffin that passes through lanes and streets,
Through day and night, with the great cloud darkening
    the land,
With the pomp of the inloop'd flags, with the cities
    draped in black,
With the show of the States themselves, as of crape-veil'd
    women, standing,
With processions long and winding, and the flambeaus of
    the night,
With the countless torches lit—with the silent sea of faces,
    and the unbared heads,

DRUM TAPS . . . .

With the waiting depot, the arriving coffin, and the som-
ber faces,
With dirges through the night, with the thousand voices
rising strong and solemn;
With all the mournful voices of the dirges, pour'd around
the coffin,
The dim-lit churches and the shuddering organs—where
amid these you journey,
With the tolling, tolling bells' perpetual clang;
Here! coffin that slowly passes,
I give you my sprig of lilac.

7

(Nor for you, for one, alone;
Blossoms and branches green to coffins all I bring:
For fresh as the morning—thus would I carol a song for
you, O sane and sacred death.

All over bouquets of roses,
O death! I cover you over with roses and early lilies;
But mostly and now the lilac that blooms the first,
Copious, I break, I break the sprigs from the bushes;
With loaded arms I come, pouring for you,
For you, and the coffins all of you, O death.)

8

O western orb, sailing the heaven!
Now I know what you must have meant as a month since
we walk'd,
As we walk'd up and down in the dark blue so mystic,
As we walk'd in silence the transparent shadowy night,

As I saw you had something to tell, as you bent to me
    night after night,
As you droop'd from the sky low down, as if to my side,
    (while the other stars all look'd on;)
As we wander'd together the solemn night, (for some-
    thing, I know not what, kept me from sleep;)
As the night advanced, and I saw on the rim of the west,
    ere you went, how full you were of woe;
As I stood on the rising ground in the breeze, in the cold
    transparent night,
As I watch'd where you pass'd and was lost in the nether-
    ward black of the night,
As my soul, in its trouble, dissatisfied, sank, as where you,
    sad orb,
Concluded, dropt in the night, and was gone.

9

Sing on, there in the swamp!
O singer bashful and tender! I hear your notes—I hear
    your call;
I hear—I come presently—I understand you;
But a moment I linger—for the lustrous star has detain'd
    me;
The star, my departing comrade, holds and detains me.

10

O how shall I warble myself for the dead one there I
    loved?
And how shall I deck my song for the large sweet soul that
    has gone?
And what shall my perfume be, for the grave of him I
    love?

DRUM TAPS . . . .

Sea-winds, blown from east and west,
Blown from the eastern sea, and blown from the western
    sea, till there on the prairies meeting:
These, and with these, and the breath of my chant,
I perfume the grave of him I love.

11

O what shall I hang on the chamber walls?
And what shall the pictures be that I hang on the walls,
To adorn the burial-house of him I love?

Pictures of growing spring, and farms, and homes,
With the Fourth-month eve at sundown, and the gray
    smoke lucid and bright,
With floods of the yellow gold of the gorgeous, indolent,
    sinking sun, burning, expanding the air;
With the fresh sweet herbage under foot, and the pale
    green leaves of the trees prolific;
In the distance the flowing glaze, the breast of the river,
    with a wind-dapple here and there;
With ranging hills on the banks, with many a line against
    the sky, and shadows;
And the city at hand, with dwellings so dense, and stacks
    of chimneys,
And all the scenes of life, and the workshops, and the
    workmen homeward returning.

12

Lo! body and soul! this land!
Mighty Manhattan, with spires, and the sparkling and
    hurrying tides, and the ships;

The varied and ample land—the South and the North in
    the light—Ohio's shores, and flashing Missouri,
And ever the far-spreading prairies, cover'd with grass and
    corn.

Lo! the most excellent sun, so calm and haughty;
The violet and purple morn, with just-felt breezes;
The gentle, soft-born, measureless light;
The miracle, spreading, bathing all—the fulfill'd noon;
The coming eve, delicious—the welcome night, and the
    stars,
Over my cities shining all, enveloping man and land.

13

Sing on! sing on, you gray-brown bird!
Sing from the swamps, the recesses—pour your chant from
    the bushes;
Limitless out of the dusk, out of the cedars and pines.

Sing on, dearest brother—warble your reedy song;
Loud human song, with voice of uttermost woe.

O liquid, and free, and tender!
O wild and loose to my soul! O wondrous singer!
You only I hear . . . yet the star holds me, (but will soon
    depart;)
Yet the lilac, with mastering odor, holds me.

14

Now while I sat in the day, and look'd forth,
In the close of the day, with its light, and the fields of
    spring, and the farmer preparing his crops,

In the large unconscious scenery of my land, with its lakes
    and forests,
In the heavenly aerial beauty, (after the perturb'd winds,
    and the storms;)
Under the arching heavens of the afternoon swift passing,
    and the voices of children and women,
The many-moving sea-tides,—and I saw the ships how
    they sail'd,
And the summer approaching with richness, and the fields
    all busy with labor,
And the infinite separate houses, how they all went on,
    each with its meals and minutia of daily usages;
And the streets, how their throbbings throbb'd, and the
    cities pent—lo! then and there,
Falling upon them all, and among them all, enveloping
    me with the rest,
Appear'd the cloud, appear'd the long black trail;
And I knew Death, its thought, and the sacred knowledge
    of death.

15

Then with the knowledge of death as walking one side of
    me,
And the thought of death close-walking the other side of
    me,
And I in the middle, as with companions, and as holding
    the hands of companions,
I fled forth to the hiding receiving night, that talks not,
Down to the shores of the water, the path by the swamp
    in the dimness,
To the solemn shadowy cedars, and ghostly pines so still.

And the singer so shy to the rest receiv'd me;
The gray-brown bird I know, receiv'd us comrades three;
And he sang what seem'd the carol of death, and a verse
for him I love.

From deep secluded recesses,
From the fragrant cedars, and the ghostly pines so still,
Came the carol of the bird.

And the charm of the carol rapt me,
As I held, as if by their hands, my comrades in the night;
And the voice of my spirit tallied the song of the bird.

DEATH CAROL

16

Come, lovely and soothing Death,
Undulate round the world, serenely arriving, arriving,
In the day, in the night, to all, to each,
Sooner or later, delicate Death.

Prais'd be the fathomless universe,
For life and joy, and for objects and knowledge curious;
And for love, sweet love—but praise! praise! praise!
For the sure-enwinding arms of cool-enfolding Death.

Dark Mother, always gliding near, with soft feet,
Have none chanted for thee a chant of fullest welcome?
Then I chant it for thee—I glorify thee above all;
I bring thee a song that when thou must indeed come,
come unfalteringly.

Approach, strong Deliveress!
When it is so—when thou hast taken them, I joyously sing
the dead,
Lost in the loving, floating ocean of thee,
Laved in the flood of thy bliss, O Death.

From me to thee glad serenades,
Dances for thee I propose, saluting thee—adornments and
feastings for thee;
And the sights of the open landscape, and the high-spread
sky, are fitting,
And life and the fields, and the huge and thoughtful night.

The night, in silence, under many a star;
The ocean shore, and the husky whispering wave, whose
voice I know:
And the soul turning to thee, O vast and well-veil'd Death,
And the body gratefully nestling close to thee.

Over the tree-tops I float thee a song!
Over the rising and sinking waves—over the myriad fields,
and the prairies wide;
Over the dense-pack'd cities all, and the teeming wharves
and ways,
I float this carol with joy, with joy to thee, O Death!

17

To the tally of my soul,
Loud and strong kept up the gray-brown bird,
With pure, deliberate notes, spreading, filling the night.

Loud in the pines and cedars dim,
Clear in the freshness moist, and the swamp-perfume;
And I with my comrades there in the night.

While my sight that was bound in my eyes unclosed,
As to long panoramas of visions.

18

I saw askant the armies;
And I saw, as in noiseless dreams, hundreds of battle-flags;
Borne through the smoke of the battles, and pierc'd with
    missiles, I saw them,
And carried hither and yon through the smoke, and torn
    and bloody;
And at last but a few shreds left on the staffs, (and all in
    silence,)
And the staffs all splinter'd and broken.

I saw battle-corpses, myriads of them,
And the white skeletons of young men—I saw them;
I saw the debris and debris of all the dead soldiers of the
    war;
But I saw they were not as was thought;
They themselves were fully at rest—they suffer'd not;
The living remain'd and suffer'd—the mother suffer'd,
And the wife and the child, and the musing comrade suf-
    fer'd,
And the armies that remain'd suffer'd.

19

Passing the visions, passing the night;
Passing, unloosing the hold of my comrades' hands;

Passing the song of the hermit bird, and the tallying song
    of my soul,
(Victorious song, death's outlet song, yet varying, ever-
    altering song,
As low and wailing, yet clear the notes, rising and falling,
    flooding the night,
Sadly sinking and fainting, as warning and warning, and
    yet again bursting with joy,
Covering the earth, and filling the spread of the heaven,
As that powerful psalm in the night I heard from recesses,
Passing, I leave thee, lilac with heart-shaped leaves;
I leave thee there in the door-yard, blooming, returning
    with spring.
I cease from my song for thee;
From my gaze on thee in the west, fronting the west, com-
    muning with thee,
O comrade lustrous, with silver face in the night.

20

Yet each I keep, and all, retrievements out of the night;
The song, the wondrous chant of the gray-brown bird,
And the tallying chant, the echo arous'd in my soul,
With the lustrous and drooping star, with the counte-
    nance full of woe,
With the lilac tall, and its blossoms of mastering odor;
With the holders holding my hand, nearing the call of the
    bird,
Comrades mine, and I in the midst, and their memory
    ever I keep—for the dead I loved so well;
For the sweetest, wisest soul of all my days and lands . . .
    and this for his dear sake;

Lilac and star and bird, twined with the chant of my
soul,
There in the fragrant pines, and the cedars dusk and dim.
1865

_____

O CAPTAIN! MY CAPTAIN!

1

O CAPTAIN! my Captain! our fearful trip is
done;
The ship has weather'd every rack, the prize we
sought is won;
The port is near, the bells I hear, the people all exulting,
While follow eyes the steady keel, the vessel grim and
daring:
But O heart! heart! heart!
O the bleeding drops of red,
Where on the deck my Captain lies,
Fallen cold and dead.

2

O Captain! my Captain! rise up and hear the bells;
Rise up—for you the flag is flung—for you the bugle trills;
For you bouquets and ribbon'd wreaths—for you the
shores a-crowding;
For you they call, the swaying mass, their eager faces turn-
ing:
Here, Captain! dear father!
This arm beneath your head;
It is some dream that on the deck,
You've fallen cold and dead.

3

My Captain does not answer, his lips are pale and still;
My father does not feel my arm, he has no pulse nor will;
The ship is anchor'd safe and sound, its voyage closed and
 done;
From fearful trip, the victor ship comes in with object
 won:
 Exult, O shores, and ring, O bells!
 But I, with mournful tread,
 Walk the deck my Captain lies,
 Fallen cold and dead. 1865

———

HUSH'D BE THE CAMPS TO-DAY

(MAY 4, 1865)

1

*H*USH'D be the camps to-day;
 And, soldiers, let us drape our war-worn
 weapons;
And each with musing soul retire, to celebrate,
Our dear commander's death.

No more for him life's stormy conflicts;
Nor victory, nor defeat—no more time's dark events,
Charging like ceaseless clouds across the sky.

2

But sing, poet, in our name;
Sing of the love we bore him—because you, dweller in
 camps, know it truly.

[64]

As they invault the coffin there;
Sing—as they close the doors of earth upon him—one
verse,
For the heavy hearts of soldiers.   1865

OLD IRELAND

*F*AR hence, amid an isle of wondrous beauty,
    Crouching over a grave, an ancient, sorrowful
        mother,
Once a queen—now lean and tatter'd, seated on the
    ground,
Her old white hair drooping dishevel'd round her shoul-
    ders;
At her feet fallen an unused royal harp,
Long silent—she too long silent—mourning her shrouded
    hope and heir;
Of all the earth her heart most full of sorrow, because
    most full of love.
Yet a word, ancient mother;
You need crouch there no longer on the cold ground, with
    forehead between your knees;
O you need not sit there, veil'd in your old white hair, so
    dishevel'd;
For know you, the one you mourn is not in that grave;
It was an illusion—the heir, the son you love, was not
    really dead;
The Lord is not dead—he is risen again, young and
    strong, in another country;

[65]

Even while you wept there by your fallen harp, by the
grave,
What you wept for, was translated, pass'd from the grave,
The winds favor'd, and the sea sail'd it,
And now with rosy and new blood,
Moves to-day in a new country.   1865

OTHERS MAY PRAISE WHAT THEY LIKE

*O*THERS may praise what they like;
    But I, from the banks of the running Missouri;
        praise nothing, in art, or aught else,
Till it has well inhaled the atmosphere of this river—also
the western prairie-scent,
And fully exudes it again.   1865

THE TORCH

*O*N my northwest coast in the midst of the night,
    a fishermen's group stands watching;
    Out on the lake, that expands before them,
        others are spearing salmon;
The canoe, a dim shadowy thing, moves across the black
water,
Bearing a Torch a-blaze at the prow.   1865

QUICKSAND YEARS

*Q*UICKSAND years that whirl me I know not
  whither,
      Your schemes, politics, fail—lines give way—
        substances mock and elude me;
Only the theme I sing, the great and strong-possess'd Soul,
    eludes not;
One's-self must never give way—that is the final substance
    —that out of all is sure;
Out of politics, triumphs, battles, life—what at last finally
    remains?
When shows break up, what but One's-Self is sure?   1865

AH, POVERTIES, WINCINGS, AND SULKY
RETREATS

*A*H, poverties, wincings, and sulky retreats!
      Ah, you foes that in conflict have overcome me!
      (For what is my life, or any man's life, but a con-
        flict with foes—the old, the incessant war?)
You degradations—you tussle with passions and appetites;
You smarts from dissatisfied friendships, (ah, wounds, the
    sharpest of all;)
You toil of painful and choked articulations—you mean-
    nesses;
You shallow tongue-talks at tables, (my tongue the shal-
    lowest of any;)

You broken resolutions, you racking angers, you smoth-
er'd ennuis;
Ah, think not you finally triumph—my real self has yet to
come forth;
It shall yet march forth o'ermastering, till all lies beneath
me;
It shall yet stand up the soldier of unquestion'd victory.

1865

WEAVE IN, WEAVE IN, MY HARDY LIFE

WEAVE in! weave in, my hardy life!
  Weave yet a soldier strong and full, for great
    campaigns to come;
Weave in red blood! weave sinews in, like ropes! the
senses, sight weave in!
Weave lasting sure! weave day and night the weft, the
warp, incessant weave! tire not!
(We know not what the use, O life! nor know the aim, the
end—nor really aught we know;
But know the work, the need goes on, and shall go on—
the death-envelop'd march of peace as well as war
goes on;)
For great campaigns of peace the same, the wiry threads to
weave;
We know not why or what, yet weave, forever weave.

1865

IN MIDNIGHT SLEEP

1

*I*N midnight sleep, of many a face of anguish,
   Of the look at first of the mortally wounded—
    of that indescribable look;
Of the dead on their backs, with arms extended wide,
   I dream, I dream, I dream.

2

Of scenes of nature, fields and mountains;
Of skies, so beauteous after a storm—and at night the
   moon so unearthly bright,
Shining sweetly, shining down, where we dig the trenches
   and gather the heaps,
   I dream, I dream, I dream.

3

Long, long have they pass'd—faces and trenches and fields;
Where through the carnage I moved with a callous com-
   posure—or away from the fallen,
Onward I sped at the time—but now of their forms at
   night,
   I dream, I dream, I dream.   1865

THICK-SPRINKLED BUNTING

*T*HICK-SPRINKLED bunting! Flag of stars!
   Long yet your road, fateful flag!—long yet your
    road, and lined with bloody death!
For the prize I see at issue, at last is the world!

All its ships and shores I see, interwoven with your
  threads, greedy banner!
—Dream'd again the flags of kings, highest born, to flaunt
  unrival'd?
O hasten, flag of man! O with sure and steady step, passing
  highest flags of kings,
Walk supreme to the heavens, mighty symbol—run up
  above the mall,
Flag of stars! thick-sprinkled bunting!   1865

YEARS OF THE MODERN

*Y*EARS of the modern! years of the unperform'd!
      Your horizon rises—I see it parting away for
      more august dramas;
I see not America only—I see not only Liberty's nation,
  but other nations preparing;
I see tremendous entrances and exits—I see new combina-
  tions—I see the solidarity of races;
I see that force advancing with irresistible power on the
  world's stage;
(Have the old forces, the old wars, played their parts? are
  the acts suitable to them closed?)
I see Freedom, completely arm'd, and victorious, and very
  haughty, with Law on one side, and Peace on the
  other,
A stupendous Trio, all issuing forth against the idea of
  caste;
—What historic dénouements are these we so rapidly approach?

[70]

I see men marching and countermarching by swift millions;

I see the frontiers and boundaries of the old aristocracies
broken;

I see the landmarks of European kings removed;

I see this day the People beginning their landmarks, (all
others give way;)

—Never were such sharp questions ask'd as this day;

Never was average man, his soul, more energetic, more
like a God;

Lo! how he urges and urges, leaving the masses no rest;

His daring foot is on land and sea everywhere—he colo-
nizes the Pacific, the archipelagoes;

With the steam-ship, the electric telegraph, the newspaper,
the wholesale engines of war,

With these, and the world-spreading factories, he inter-
links all geography, all lands;

—What whispers are these, O lands, running ahead of you,
passing under the seas?

Are all nations communing? is there going to be but one
heart to the globe?

Is humanity forming, en-masse?—for lo! tyrants tremble,
crowns grow dim;

The earth, restive, confronts a new era, perhaps a general
divine war;

No one knows what will happen next—such portents fill
the days and nights;

Years prophetical! the space ahead as I walk, as I vainly
try to pierce it, is full of phantoms;

Unborn deeds, things soon to be, project their shapes
around me;

This incredible rush and heat—this strange ecstatic fever
of dreams, O years!
Your dreams, O years, how they penetrate through me! (I
know not whether I sleep or wake!)
The perform'd America and Europe grow dim, retiring in
shadow behind me,
The unperform'd, more gigantic than ever, advance, advance upon me.   1865

ASHES OF SOLDIERS

ASHES of soldiers!
        As I muse, retrospective, murmuring a chant in
            thought,
Lo! the war resumes—again to my sense your shapes,
And again the advance of armies.

Noiseless as mists and vapors,
From their graves in the trenches ascending,
From the cemeteries all through Virginia and Tennessee,
From every point of the compass, out of the countless un-
named graves,
In wafted clouds, in myriads large, or squads of twos or
threes, or single ones, they come,
And silently gather round me.

Now sound no note, O trumpeters!
Not at the head of my cavalry, parading on spirited horses,
With sabers drawn and glist'ning, and carbines by their
thighs— (ah, my brave horsemen!

. . . . DRUM TAPS

My handsome, tan-faced horsemen! what life, what joy
  and pride,
With all the perils, were yours!)

Nor you drummers—neither at reveille, at dawn,
Nor the long roll alarming the camp—nor even the muf-
  fled beat for a burial;
Nothing from you, this time, O drummers, bearing my
  war-like drums.
But aside from these, and the marts of wealth, and the
  crowded promenade,
Admitting around me comrades close, unseen by the rest,
  and voiceless,
The slain elate and alive again—the dust and debris alive,
I chant this chant of my silent soul, in the name of all
  dead soldiers.

Faces so pale, with wondrous eyes, very dear, gather closer
  yet;
Draw close, but speak not.

Phantoms of countless lost!
Invisible to the rest, henceforth become my companions!
Follow me ever! desert me not, while I live.

Sweet are the blooming cheeks of the living! sweet are the
  musical voices sounding!
But sweet, ah sweet, are the dead, with their silent eyes.

Dearest comrades! all is over and long gone;
But love is not over—and what love, O comrades!
Perfume from battle-fields rising—up from fœtor arising.

[73]

Perfume therefore my chant, O love! immortal Love!
Give me to bathe the memories of all dead soldiers,
Shroud them, embalm them, cover them all over with
tender pride!

Perfume all! make all wholesome!
Make these ashes to nourish and blossom,
O love! O chant! solve all, fructify all with the last chem-
istry.

Give me exhaustless—make me a fountain,
That I exhale love from me wherever I go, like a moist
perennial dew,
For the ashes of all dead soldiers.   1865

PENSIVE, ON HER DEAD GAZING, I HEARD THE MOTHER OF ALL

*P*ENSIVE, on her dead gazing, I heard the Mother
of All,
Desperate, on the torn bodies, on the forms
covering the battle-fields gazing;
(As the last gun ceased—but the scent of the powder-
smoke linger'd;)
As she call'd to her earth with mournful voice while she
stalk'd:
Absorb them well, O my earth, she cried—I charge you,
lose not my sons! lose not an atom;
And you streams, absorb them well, taking their dear
blood;

And you local spots, and you airs that swim above lightly,
And all you essences of soil and growth—and you, my
rivers' depths;
And you mountain sides—and the woods where my dear
children's blood, trickling, redden'd;
And you trees, down in your roots, to bequeath to all fu-
ture trees,
My dead absorb—my young men's beautiful bodies absorb
—and their precious, precious, precious blood;
Which holding in trust for me, faithfully back again give
me, many a year hence,
In unseen essence and odor of surface and grass, centuries
hence;
In blowing airs from the fields, back again give me my darlings—give my immortal heroes;
Exhale me them centuries hence—breathe me their breath
—let not an atom be lost;
O years and graves! O air and soil! O my dead, an aroma
sweet!
Exhale them perennial, sweet death, years, centuries
hence.   1865

CAMPS OF GREEN

NOT alone those camps of white, O soldiers,
    When, as order'd forward, after a long march,
    Footsore and weary, soon as the light lessen'd, we
        halted for the night;
Some of us so fatigued, carrying the gun and knapsack,
    dropping asleep in our tracks;

Others pitching the little tents, and the fires lit up began
    to sparkle;
Outposts of pickets posted, surrounding, alert through the
    dark,
And a word provided for countersign, careful for safety;
Till to the call of the drummers at daybreak loudly beat-
    ing the drums,
We rose up refresh'd, the night and sleep pass'd over, and
    resumed our journey,
Or proceeded to battle.
Lo! the camps of the tents of green,
Which the days of peace keep filling, and the days of war
    keep filling,
With a mystic army, (is it too order'd forward? is it too
    only halting awhile,
Till night and sleep pass over?)

Now in those camps of green—in their tents dotting the
    world;
In the parents, children, husbands, wives, in them—in the
    old and young,
Sleeping under the sunlight, sleeping under the moon-
    light, content and silent there at last,
Behold the mighty bivouac-field, and waiting-camp of
    all.
Of corps and generals all, and the President over the corps
    and generals all,
And of each of us, O soldiers, and of each and all in the
    ranks we fought,
(There without hatred we shall all meet.)

For presently, O soldiers, we too camp in our place in the
    bivouac-camps of green;
But we need not provide for outposts, nor word for the
    countersign,
Nor drummer to beat the morning drum.   1865

I HEARD YOU, SOLEMN-SWEET PIPES OF
THE ORGAN

I HEARD you, solemn-sweet pipes of the organ, as
    last Sunday morn I pass'd the church;
    Winds of autumn!—as I walk'd the woods at
dusk, I heard your long-stretch'd sighs, up above, so
mournful;
I heard the perfect Italian tenor, singing at the opera—I
    heard the soprano in the midst of the quartet singing;
. . . Heart of my love! you too I heard, murmuring low,
    through one of the wrists around my head;
Heard the pulse of you, when all was still, ringing little
    bells last night under my ear.   1865

CHANTING THE SQUARE DEIFIC

1

CHANTING the square deific, out of the One ad-
    vancing, out of the sides;
    Out of the old and new—out of the square en-
tirely divine,
Solid, four-sided, (all the sides needed) . . . from this
    side JEHOVAH am I,

[77]

Old Brahm I, and I Saturnius am;
Not Time affects me—I am Time, old, modern as any;
Unpersuadable, relentless, executing righteous judgments;
As the Earth, the Father, the brown old Kronos, with laws,
Aged beyond computation—yet ever new—ever with
    those mighty laws rolling,
Relentless, I forgive no man—whoever sins, dies—I will
    have that man's life;
Therefore let none expect mercy—have the seasons, gravi-
    tation, the appointed days, mercy?—no more have I;
But as the seasons, and gravitation—and as all the ap-
    pointed days, that forgive not,
I dispense from this side judgments inexorable, without
    the least remorse.

2

Consolator most mild, the promis'd one advancing,
With gentle hand extended—the mightier God am I,
Foretold by prophets and poets, in their most rapt prophe-
    cies and poems;
From this side, lo! the Lord CHRIST gazes—lo! Hermes I—
    lo! mine is Hercules' face;
All sorrow, labor, suffering, I, tallying it, absorb in myself;
Many times have I been rejected, taunted, put in prison,
    and crucified—and many times shall be again;
All the world have I given up for my dear brothers' and
    sisters' sake—for the soul's sake;
Wending my way through the homes of men, rich or poor,
    with the kiss of affection;
For I am affection—I am the cheer-bringing God, with
    hope, and all-enclosing Charity;

(Conqueror yet—for before me all the armies and soldiers
    of the earth shall yet bow—and all the weapons of war
    become impotent:)
With indulgent words, as to children—with fresh and
    sane words, mine only;
Young and strong I pass, knowing well I am destin'd my-
    self to an early death:
But my Charity has no death—my Wisdom dies not,
    neither early nor late,
And my sweet Love, bequeath'd here and elsewhere, never
    dies.

3

Aloof, dissatisfied, plotting revolt,
Comrade of criminals, brother of slaves,
Crafty, despised, a drudge, ignorant,
With sudra face and worn brow, black, but in the depths
    of my heart, proud as any;
Lifted, now and always, against whoever, scorning, as-
    sumes to rule me;
Morose, full of guile, full of reminiscences, brooding, with
    many wiles,
(Though it was thought I was baffled and dispell'd, and
    my wiles done—but that will never be;)
Defiant, I, SATAN, still live—still utter words—in new
    lands duly appearing, (and old ones also;)
Permanent here, from my side, warlike, equal with any,
    real as any,
Nor time, nor change, shall ever change me or my
    words.

4

Santa SPIRITA, breather, life,
Beyond the light, lighter than light,
Beyond the flames of hell—joyous, leaping easily above
    hell;
Beyond Paradise—perfumed solely with mine own per-
    fume;
Including all life on earth—touching, including God—in-
    cluding Saviour and Satan;
Ethereal, pervading all, (for without me, what were all?
    what were God?)
Essence of forms—life of the real identities, permanent,
    positive, (namely the unseen,)
Life of the great round world, the sun and stars, and of
    man—I, the general Soul,
Here the square finishing, the solid, I the most solid,
Breath my breath also through these songs.   1865

ONE'S-SELF I SING

ONE'S-SELF I sing—a simple, separate Person;
    Yet utter the word Democratic, the word En-
    masse.

Of Physiology from top to toe I sing;
Not physiognomy alone, nor brain alone, is worthy for the
    muse—I say the Form complete is worthier far;
The Female equally with the male I sing.

Of Life immense in passion, pulse, and power,
Cheerful—for freest action form'd, under the laws divine,
The Modern Man I sing.   1867

[80]

WHEN I READ THE BOOK

WHEN I read the book, the biography famous,
        And is this, then, (said I,) what the author
            calls a man's life?
And so will some one, when I am dead and gone, write
    my life?
As if any man really knew aught of my life;
Why, even I myself, I often think, know little or nothing
    of my real life;
Only a few hints—a few diffused, faint clues and indirec-
    tions,
I seek, for my own use, to trace out here.   1867

BEGINNING MY STUDIES

BEGINNING my studies, the first step pleas'd me
        so much,
        The mere fact, consciousness—these forms—the
            power of motion,
The least insect or animal—the senses—eyesight—love;
The first step, I say, aw'd me and pleas'd me so much,
I have hardly gone, and hardly wish'd to go, any farther,
But stop and loiter all the time, to sing it in ecstatic songs.
                                                    1867

[81]

SHUT NOT YOUR DOORS, Etc.

SHUT not your doors to me, proud libraries,
    For that which was lacking on all your well-
       fill'd shelves, yet needed most, I bring;
Forth from the army, the war emerging—a book I have
    made,
The words of my book nothing—the drift of it everything;
A book separate, not link'd with the rest, nor felt by the
    intellect,
But you, ye untold latencies, will thrill to every page;
Through Space and Time fused in a chant, and the flow-
    ing, eternal Identity,
To Nature, encompassing these, encompassing God—to
    the joyous, electric All,
To the sense of Death—and accepting, exulting in Death,
    in its turn, the same as life,
The entrance of Man I sing.   1867

TEARS

TEARS! tears! tears!
    In the night, in solitude, tears;
       On the white shore dripping, dripping, suck'd
       in by the sand;
Tears—not a star shining—all dark and desolate;
Moist tears from the eyes of a muffled head:
—O who is that ghost?—that form in the dark, with tears?

What shapeless lump is that, bent, crouch'd there on the
    sand?
Streaming tears—sobbing tears—throes, choked with wild
    cries;
O storm, embodied, rising, careering, with swift steps
    along the beach;
O wild and dismal night storm, with wind! O belching
    and desperate!
O shade, so sedate and decorous by day, with calm coun-
    tenance and regulated pace;
But away at night, as you fly, none looking—O then the
    unloosen'd ocean,
Of tears! tears! tears!   1867

ABOARD, AT A SHIP'S HELM

ABOARD, at a ship's helm,
    A young steersman, steering with care.

A bell through fog on a sea-coast dolefully ringing,
An ocean-bell—O a warning bell, rock'd by the waves.
O you give good notice indeed, you bell by the sea-reefs
    ringing,
Ringing, ringing, to warn the ship from its wreck-place.

For, as on the alert, O steersman, you mind the bell's
    admonition,
The bows turn,—the freighted ship, tacking, speeds away
    under her gray sails,
The beautiful and noble ship, with all her precious
    wealth, speeds away gaily and safe.

[83]

But O the ship, the immortal ship! O ship aboard the
ship!
O ship of the body—ship of the soul—voyaging, voyaging,
voyaging.   1867

THE RUNNER

ON a flat road runs the well-train'd runner;
He is lean and sinewy, with muscular legs;
He is thinly clothed—he leans forward as he runs,
With lightly closed fists, and arms partially rais'd.   1867

THE CITY DEAD-HOUSE

BY the City Dead-House, by the gate,
As idly sauntering, wending my way from the
clangor,
I curious pause—for lo! an outcast form, a poor dead pros-
titute brought;
Her corpse they deposit unclaim'd—it lies on the damp
brick pavement;
The divine woman, her body—I see the Body—I look on
it alone,
That house once full of passion and beauty—all else I
notice not;
Nor stillness so cold, nor running water from faucet, nor
odors morbific impress me;
But the house alone—that wondrous house—that delicate
fair house—that ruin!

That immortal house, more than all the rows of dwellings
    ever built!
Or white-domed Capitol itself, with majestic figure sur-
    mounted—or all the old high-spired cathedrals;
That little house alone, more than them all—poor, desper-
    ate house!
Fair, fearful wreck! tenement of a Soul! itself a Soul!
Unclaim'd, avoided house! take one breath from my trem-
    ulous lips;
Take one tear, dropt aside as I go, for thought of you,
Dead house of love! house of madness and sin, crumbled!
    crush'd!
House of life—erewhile talking and laughing—but ah,
    poor house! dead, even then;
Months, years, an echoing, garnish'd house—but dead,
    dead, dead.   1867

_____

INSCRIPTION

*S*MALL is the theme of the following Chant, yet
    the greatest—namely, One's-Self—that won-
    drous thing a simple, separate person. That,
for the use of the New World, I sing.
Man's physiology complete, from top to toe, I sing. Not
    physiognomy alone, nor brain alone, is worthy for the
    muse; I say the Form complete is worthier far. The
    female equal with the male, I sing,
Nor cease at the theme of One's-Self. I speak the word of
    the modern, the word En-Masse:
My Days I sing, and the Lands—with interstice I knew of
    hapless War.

[85]

O friend whoe'er you are, at last arriving hither to com-
mence, I feel through every leaf the pressure of your
hand, which I return. And thus upon our journey
link'd together let us go.   1867

A CAROL OF HARVEST, FOR 1867

1

A SONG of the good green grass!
A song no more of the city streets;
A song of farms—a song of the soil of fields.

A song with the smell of sun-dried hay, where the nimble
pitchers handle the pitch-fork;
A song tasting of new wheat, and of fresh-husk'd maize.

2

For the lands, and for these passionate days, and for my-
self,
Now I awhile return to thee, O soil of Autumn fields,
Reclining on thy breast, giving myself to thee,
Answering the pulses of thy sane and equable heart,
Tuning a verse for thee.

O Earth, that hast no voice, confide to me a voice!
O harvest of my lands! O boundless summer growths!
O lavish, brown, parturient earth! O infinite, teeming
womb!
A verse to seek, to see, to narrate thee.

[86]

3

Ever upon this stage,
Is acted God's calm, annual drama,
Gorgeous processions, songs of birds,
Sunrise, that fullest feeds and freshens most the soul,
The heaving sea, the waves upon the shore, the musical,
     strong waves,
The woods, the stalwart trees, the slender, tapering trees,
The flowers, the grass, the lilliput, countless armies of the
     grass,
The heat, the showers, the measureless pasturages,
The scenery of the snows, the winds' free orchestra,
The stretching, light-hung roof of clouds—the clear ceru-
     lean, and the bulging, silvery fringes,
The high dilating stars, the placid, beckoning stars,
The moving flocks and herds, the plains and emerald
     meadows,
The shows of all the varied lands, and all the growths and
     products.

4

Fecund America! To-day,
Thou art all over set in births and joys!
Thou groan'st with riches! thy wealth clothes thee as with
     a swathing garment!
Thou laughest loud with ache of great possessions!
A myriad-twining life, like interlacing vines, binds all thy
     vast demesne!
As some huge ship, freighted to water's edge, thou ridest
     into port!

As rain falls from the heaven, and vapors rise from earth,
    so have the precious values fallen upon thee, and
    risen out of thee!
Thou envy of the globe! thou miracle!
Thou, bathed, choked, swimming in plenty!
Thou lucky Mistress of the tranquil barns!
Thou Prairie Dame that sittest in the middle, and lookest
    out upon thy world, and lookest East, and lookest
    West!
Dispensatress, that by a word givest a thousand miles—
    that giv'st a million farms, and missest nothing!
Thou All-Acceptress—thou Hospitable— (thou only art
    hospitable, as God is hospitable.)

5

When late I sang, sad was my voice;
Sad were the shows around me, with deafening noises of
    hatred, and smoke of conflict;
In the midst of the armies, the Heroes, I stood,
Or pass'd with slow step through the wounded and dying.

But now I sing not War,
Nor the measur'd march of soldiers, nor the tents of
    camps,
Nor the regiments hastily coming up, deploying in line of
    battle.

No more the dead and wounded;
No more the sad, unnatural shows of War.

Ask'd room those flush'd immortal ranks? the first forth-
    stepping armies?
Ask room, alas, the ghastly ranks—the armies dread that
    follow'd.

6

(Pass—pass, ye proud brigades!
So handsome, dress'd in blue—with your tramping,
    sinewy legs;
With your shoulders young and strong—with your knap-
    sacks and your muskets;
How elate I stood and watch'd you, where, starting off,
    you march'd!

Pass;—then rattle, drums, again!
Scream, you steamers on the river, out of whistles loud
    and shrill, your salutes!
For an army heaves in sight—O another gathering army!
Swarming, trailing on the rear—O you dread, accruing
    army!
O you regiments so piteous, with your mortal diarrhœa!
    with your fever!
O my land's maimed darlings! with the plenteous bloody
    bandage and the crutch!
Lo! your pallid army follow'd!)

7

But on these days of brightness,
On the far-stretching beauteous landscape, the roads and
    lanes, the high-piled farm-wagons, and the fruits and
    barns,
Shall the dead intrude?

Ah, the dead to me mar not—they fit well in Nature;
They fit very well in the landscape, under the trees and
grass,
And along the edge of the sky, in the horizon's far margin.

Nor do I forget you, departed;
Nor in winter or summer, my lost ones;
But most, in the open air, as now, when my soul is rapt
and at peace—like pleasing phantoms,
Your dear memories, rising, glide silently by me.

8

I saw the day, the return of the Heroes;
(Yet the Heroes never surpass'd, sha¹l never return;
Them, that day, I saw not.)

I saw the interminable Corps—I saw the processions of
armies,
I saw them approaching, defiling by, with divisions,
Streaming northward, their work done, camping awhile in
clusters of mighty camps.

No holiday soldiers!—youthful, yet veterans;
Worn, swart, handsome, strong, of the stock of homestead
and workshop,
Harden'd of many a long campaign and sweaty march,
Inured on many a hard-fought, bloody field.

9

A pause—the armies wait;
A million flush'd, embattled conquerors wait;

The world, too, waits—then, soft as breaking night, and
    sure as dawn,
They melt—they disappear.

Exult, indeed, O lands! victorious lands!
Not there your victory, on those red, shuddering fields;
But here and hence your victory.

Melt, melt away, ye armies! disperse, ye blue-clad soldiers!
Resolve ye back again—give up, for good, your deadly
    arms;
Other the arms, the fields henceforth for you, or South or
    North, or East or West,
With saner wars—sweet wars—life-giving wars.

10

Loud, O my throat, and clear, O soul!
The season of thanks, and the voice of full-yielding;
The chant of joy and power for boundless fertility.

All till'd and untill'd fields expand before me;
I see the true arenas of my race—or first, or last,
Man's innocent and strong arenas.

I see the Heroes at other toils;
I see, well-wielded in their hands, the better weapons.

11

I see where America, Mother of All,
Well-pleased, with full-spanning eye, gazes forth, dwells
    long,
And counts the varied gathering of the products.

Busy the far, the sunlit panorama;
Prairie, orchard, and yellow grain of the North,
Cotton and rice of the South, and Louisianian cane;
Open, unseeded fallows, rich fields of clover and timothy,
Kine and horses feeding, and droves of sheep and swine,
And many a stately river flowing, and many a jocund
brook,
And healthy uplands with their herby-perfumed breezes,
And the good green grass—that delicate miracle, the ever-
recurring grass.

12

Toil on, Heroes! harvest the products!
Not alone on those warlike fields, the Mother of All,
With dilated form and lambent eyes, watch'd you.

Toil on, Heroes! toil well! Handle the weapons well!
The Mother of All—yet here, as ever, she watches you.

Well-pleased, America, thou beholdest,
Over the fields of the West, those crawling monsters,
The human-divine inventions, the labor-saving imple-
ments:
Beholdest, moving in every direction, imbued as with life,
the revolving hay-rakes,
The steam-power reaping-machines, and the horse-power
machines,
The engines, thrashers of grain, and cleaners of grain, well
separating the straw—the nimble work of the patent
pitch-fork;
Beholdest the newer saw-mill, the southern cotton-gin,
and the rice-cleanser.

Beneath thy look, O Maternal,
With these, and else, and with their own strong hands, the
    Heroes harvest.
All gather, and all harvest;
(Yet but for thee, O Powerful! not a scythe might swing,
    as now, in security;
Not a maize-stalk dangle, as now, its silken tassels in
    peace.)

13

Under Thee only they harvest—even but a wisp of hay,
    under thy great face, only;
Harvest the wheat of Ohio, Illinois, Wisconsin—every
    barked spear, under thee;
Harvest the maize of Missouri, Kentucky, Tennessee—
    each ear in its light-green sheath,
Gather the hay to its myriad mows, in the odorous, tran-
    quil barns,
Oats to their bins—the white potato, the buckwheat of
    Michigan, to theirs;
Gather the cotton in Mississippi or Alabama—dig and
    hoard the golden, the sweet potato of Georgia and
    the Carolinas,
Clip the wool of California or Pennsylvania,
Cut the flax in the Middle States, or hemp, or tobacco in
    the Borders,
Pick the pea and the bean, or pull apples from the trees,
    or bunches of grapes from the vines,
Or aught that ripens in all These States, or North or
    South,
Under the beaming sun, and under Thee.   1867

DRUM TAPS . . . .

DAREST THOU NOW, O SOUL

1

*D*AREST thou now, O Soul,
Walk out with me toward the Unknown Region,
Where neither ground is for the feet, nor any
path to follow?

2

No map, there, nor guide,
Nor voice sounding, nor touch of human hand,
Nor face with blooming flesh, nor lips, nor eyes, are in
that land.

3

I know it not, O Soul;
Nor dost thou—all is a blank before us;
All waits, undream'd of, in that region—that inaccessible
land.

4

Till, when the ties loosen,
All but the ties eternal, Time and Space,
Nor darkness, gravitation, sense, nor any bounds, bound
us.

5

Then we burst forth—we float,
In Time and Space, O Soul—prepared for them;
Equal, equipt at last— (O joy! O fruit of all!) them to
fulfil, O Soul.   1868

[94]

WHISPERS OF HEAVENLY DEATH

WHISPERS of heavenly death, murmur'd I hear;
Labial gossip of night—sibilant chorals;
Footsteps gently ascending—mystical breezes,
wafted soft and low;
Ripples of unseen rivers—tides of a current, flowing, for-
ever flowing;
(Or is it the plashing of tears? the measureless waters of
human tears?)
I see, just see, skyward, great cloud-masses;
Mournfully, slowly they roll, silently swelling and mixing;
With, at times, a half-dimm'd, sadden'd, far-off star,
Appearing and disappearing.

(Some parturition, rather—some solemn, immortal birth:
On the frontiers, to eyes impenetrable,
Some Soul is passing over.)   1868

A NOISELESS, PATIENT SPIDER

A NOISELESS, patient spider,
I mark'd, where, on a little promontory, it stood.
isolated;
Mark'd how, to explore the vacant, vast surrounding,
It launch'd forth filament, filament, filament, out of itself;
Ever unreeling them—ever tirelessly speeding them.

And you, O my Soul, where you stand,
Surrounded, surrounded, in measureless oceans of space,

Ceaselessly musing, venturing, throwing,—seeking the
    spheres, to connect them;
Till the bridge you will need, be form'd—till the ductile
    anchor hold;
Till the gossamer thread you fling, catch somewhere, O
    my Soul.   1868

PENSIVE AND FALTERING

*P*ENSIVE and faltering,
    The words, *the dead,* I write;
    For living are the Dead;
(Haply the only living, only real,
And I the apparition—I the specter.)   1868

THE LAST INVOCATION

1

*A*T the last, tenderly,
    From the walls of the powerful, fortress'd house,
    From the clasp of the knitted locks—from the
        keep of the well-closed doors,
Let me be wafted.

2

Let me glide noiselessly forth;
With the key of softness unlock the locks—with a whisper,
Set ope the doors, O Soul!

[96]

3

Tenderly! be not impatient!
(Strong is your hold, O mortal flesh!
Strong is your hold, O love.) 1868

―――――

PROUD MUSIC OF THE STORM

1

*P*ROUD music of the storm!
      Blast that careers so free, whistling across the
            prairies!
Strong hum of forest tree-tops! Wind of the mountains!
Personified dim shapes! you hidden orchestras!
You serenades of phantoms, with instruments alert,
Blending, with Nature's rhythmus, all the tongues of
      nations;
You chords left us by vast composers! you choruses!
You formless, free, religious dances! you from the Orient!
You undertone of rivers, roar of pouring cataracts;
You sounds from distant guns, with galloping cavalry!
Echoes of camps, with all the different bugle-calls!
Trooping tumultuous, filling the midnight late, bending
      me powerless,
Entering my lonesome slumber-chamber—why have you
      seiz'd me?

2

Come forward, O my Soul, and let the rest retire;
Listen—lose not—it is toward thee they tend;

Parting the midnight, entering my slumber-chamber,
For thee they sing and dance, O Soul.
A festival song!
The duet of the bridegroom and the bride—a marriage-
    march,
With lips of love, and hearts of lovers, fill'd to the brim
    with love;
The red-flush'd cheeks, and perfumes—the cortege
    swarming, full of friendly faces, young and old,
To flutes' clear notes, and sounding harps' cantabile.

3

Now loud approaching drums!
Victoria! see'st thou in powder-smoke the banners torn
    but flying? the rout of the baffled?
Hearest those shouts of a conquering army?

(Ah, Soul, the sobs of women—the wounded groaning in
    agony,
The hiss and crackle of flames—the blacken'd ruins—
    the embers of cities,
The dirge and desolation of mankind.)

4

Now airs antique and medieval fill me!
I see and hear old harpers with their harps, at Welsh
    festivals:
I hear the minnesingers, singing their lays of love,
I hear the minstrels, gleemen, troubadours, of the feudal
    ages.

5

Now the great organ sounds,
Tremulous—while underneath, (as the hid footholds of
    the earth,
On which arising, rest, and leaping forth, depend,
All shapes of beauty, grace and strength—all hues we
    know,
Green blades of grass, and warbling birds—children that
    gambol and play—the clouds of heaven above,)
The strong bass stands, and its pulsations intermit not,
Bathing, supporting, merging all the rest—maternity of
    all the rest;
And with it every instrument in multitudes,
The players playing—all the world's musicians,
The solemn hymns and masses, rousing adoration,
All passionate heart-chants, sorrowful appeals,
The measureless sweet vocalists of ages,
And for their solvent setting, Earth's own diapason,
Of winds and woods and mighty ocean waves;
A new composite orchestra—binder of years and climes
    —ten-fold renewer,
As of the far-back days the poets tell—the Paradiso,
The straying thence, the separation long, but now the
    wandering done,
The journey done, the Journeyman come home,
And Man and Art, with Nature fused again.

6

Tutti! for Earth and Heaven!
The Almighty Leader now for me, for once has signal'd
    with his wand.

The manly strophe of the husbands of the world,
And all the wives responding.
The tongues of violins!
(I think, O tongues, ye tell this heart, that cannot tell
    itself;
This brooding, yearning heart, that cannot tell itself.)

7

Ah, from a little child,
Thou knowest, Soul, how to me all sounds became music;
My mother's voice, in lullaby or hymn;
(The voice—O tender voices—memory's loving voices!
Last miracle of all—O dearest mother's, sister's, voices;)
The rain, the growing corn, the breeze among the long-
    leav'd corn,
The measur'd sea-surf, beating on the sand,
The twittering bird, the hawk's sharp scream,
The wild-fowl's notes at night, as flying low, migrating
    north or south,
The psalm in the country church, or mid the clustering
    trees, the open air camp-meeting,
The fiddler in the tavern—the glee, the long-strung
    sailor-song,
The lowing cattle, bleating sheep—the crowing cock at
    dawn.

8

All songs of current lands come sounding 'round me,
The German airs of friendship, wine and love,
Irish ballads, merry jigs and dances—English warbles,
Chansons of France, Scotch tunes—and o'er the rest,
Italia's peerless compositions.

[100]

Across the stage, with pallor on her face, yet lurid passion,
Stalks Norma, brandishing the dagger in her hand.

I see poor crazed Lucia's eyes' unnatural gleam;
Her hair down her back falls loose and dishevel'd.
I see where Ernani, walking the bridal garden,
Amid the scent of night-roses, radiant, holding his bride
      by the hand,
Hears the infernal call, the death-pledge of the horn.

To crossing swords, and gray hairs bared to heaven,
The clear, electric base and baritone of the world,
The trombone duo—Libertad forever!

From Spanish chestnut trees' dense shade,
By old and heavy convent walls, a wailing song,
Song of lost love—the torch of youth and life quench'd
      in despair,
Song of the dying swan—Fernando's heart is breaking.

Awaking from her woes at last, retriev'd Amina sings;
Copious as stars, and glad as morning light, the torrents
      of her joy.

(The teeming lady comes!
The lustrous orb—Venus contralto—the blooming
      mother,
Sister of loftiest gods—Alboni's self I hear.)

9

I hear those odes, symphonies, operas;
I hear in the *William Tell,* the music of an arous'd and
      angry people;

[101]

I hear Meyerbeer's *Huguenots,* the *Prophet,* or *Robert;*
Gounod's *Faust,* or Mozart's *Don Juan.*

10

I hear the dance-music of all nations,
The waltz, (some delicious measure, lapsing, bathing me
    in bliss;)
The bolero, to tinkling guitars and clattering castanets.
I see religious dances old and new,
I hear the sound of the Hebrew lyre,
I see the Crusaders marching, bearing the cross on high,
    to the martial clang of cymbals;
I hear dervishes monotonously chanting, interspers'd with
    frantic shouts, as they spin around, turning always
    towards Mecca;
I see the rapt religious dances of the Persians and the
    Arabs;
Again, at Eleusis, home of Ceres, I see the modern Greeks
    dancing,
I hear them clapping their hands, as they bend their bodies,
I hear the metrical shuffling of their feet.

I see again the wild old Corybantian dance, the perform-
    ers wounding each other;
I see the Roman youth, to the shrill sound of flageolets,
    throwing and catching their weapons,
As they fall on their knees, and rise again.
I hear from the Mussulman mosque the muezzin calling;
I see the worshipers within, (nor form, nor sermon, argu-
    ment, nor word,
But silent, strange, devout—rais'd, glowing heads—ec-
    static faces.)

11

I hear the Egyptian harp of many strings,
The primitive chants of the Nile boatmen;
The sacred imperial hymns of China,
To the delicate sounds of the king, (the stricken wood
    and stone;)
Or to Hindu flutes, and the fretting twang of the vina,
A band of bayaderes.

12

Now Asia, Africa leave me—Europe, seizing, inflates me;
To organs huge, and bands, I hear as from vast con-
    courses of voices,
Luther's strong hymn, *Eine feste Burg ist unser Gott;*
Rossini's *Stabat Mater dolorosa;*
Or, floating in some high cathedral dim, with gorgeous
    color'd windows,
The passionate *Agnus Dei,* or *Gloria in Excelsis.*

13

Composers! mighty maestros!
And you, sweet singers of old lands—Soprani! Tenori!
    Bassi!
To you a new bard, caroling free in the west,
Obeisant, sends his love.

(Such led to thee, O Soul!
All senses, shows and objects, lead to thee,
But now, it seems to me, sound leads o'er all the rest.)

14

I hear the annual singing of the children in St. Paul's
 Cathedral;
Or, under the high roof of some colossal hall, the sym-
 phonies, oratorios of Beethoven, Handel, or Haydn;
The *Creation,* in billows of godhood laves me.

Give me to hold all sounds, (I, madly struggling, cry,)
Fill me with all the voices of the universe,
Endow me with their throbbings—Nature's also,
The tempests, waters, winds—operas and chants—marches
 and dances,
Utter—pour in—for I would take them all.

15

Then I woke softly,
And pausing, questioning awhile the music of my dream,
And questioning all those reminiscences—the tempest in
 its fury,
And all the songs of sopranos and tenors,
And those rapt Oriental dances, of religious fervor,
And the sweet varied instruments, and the diapason of
 organs,
And all the artless plaints of love, and grief and death,
I said to my silent, curious Soul, out of the bed of the
 slumber-chamber,
Come, for I have found the clue I sought so long,
Let us go forth refresh'd amid the day,
Cheerfully tallying life, walking the world, the real,
Nourish'd henceforth by our celestial dream.

And I said, moreover,
Haply, what thou hast heard, O Soul, was not the sound of
    winds,
Nor dream of raging storm, nor sea-hawk's flapping wings,
    nor harsh scream,
Nor vocalism of sun-bright Italy,
Nor German organ majestic—nor vast concourse of voices
    —nor layers of harmonies;
Nor strophes of husbands and wives—nor sound of march-
    ing soldiers,
Nor flutes, nor harps, nor the bugle-calls of camps;
But, to a new rhythmus fitted for thee,
Poems, bridging the way from Life to Death, vaguely
    wafted in night air, uncaught, unwritten,
Which, let us go forth in the bold day, and write.   1868

THE SINGER IN THE PRISON

1

O sight of shame, and pain, and dole!
O fearful thought—a convict Soul!

RANG the refrain along the hall, the prison,
    Rose to the roof, the vaults of heaven above,
    Pouring in floods of melody, in tones so pensive,
        sweet and strong, the like whereof was
    never heard,
Reaching the far-off sentry, and the armed guards, who
    ceas'd their pacing,
Making the hearer's pulses stop for ecstasy and awe.

2

O sight of pity, gloom, and dole!
O pardon me, a hapless Soul!

The sun was low in the west one winter day,
When down a narrow aisle, amid the thieves and outlaws
 of the land,
(There by the hundreds seated, sear-faced murderers, wily
 counterfeiters,
Gather'd to Sunday church in prison walls—the keepers
 round,
Plenteous, well-arm'd, watching, with vigilant eyes,)
All that dark, cankerous blotch, a nation's criminal mass,
Calmly a Lady walk'd, holding a little innocent child by
 either hand,
Whom, seating on their stools beside her on the platform,
She, first preluding with the instrument, a low and musi-
 cal prelude,
In voice surpassing all, sang forth a quaint old hymn.

3

THE HYMN

A Soul, confined by bars and bands,
Cries, Help! O help! and wrings her hands;
Blinded her eyes—bleeding her breast,
Nor pardon finds, nor balm of rest.

O sight of shame, and pain, and dole!
O fearful thought—a convict Soul!

Ceaseless, she paces to and fro;
O heart-sick days! O nights of wo!
Nor hand of friend, nor loving face;
Nor favor comes, nor word of grace.

O sight of pity, gloom, and dole!
O pardon me, a helpless Soul!

It was not I that sinn'd the sin,
The ruthless Body dragg'd me in;
Though long I strove courageously,
The Body was too much for me.

O Life! no life, but bitter dole!
O burning, beaten, baffled Soul!

(Dear prison'd Soul, bear up a space,
For soon or late the certain grace;
To set thee free, and bear thee home,
The Heavenly Pardoner Death shall come.

Convict no more—nor shame, nor dole!
Depart! a God-enfranchis'd Soul!)

4

The singer ceas'd;
One glance swept from her clear, calm eyes, o'er all those
    upturn'd faces;
Strange sea of prison faces—a thousand varied, crafty,
    brutal, seam'd and beauteous faces;
Then rising, passing back along the narrow aisle between
    them,
While her gown touch'd them, rustling in the silence,
She vanish'd with her children in the dusk.

5

While upon all, convicts and armed keepers, ere they
    stirr'd,
(Convict forgetting prison, keeper his loaded pistol,)
A hush and pause fell down, a wondrous minute,
With deep, half-stifled sobs, and sound of bad men bow'd,
    and moved to weeping,
And youth's convulsive breathings, memories of home,
The mother's voice in lullaby, the sister's care, the happy
    childhood,
The long-pent spirit rous'd to reminiscence;
—A wondrous minute then—but after, in the solitary
    night, to many, many there,
Years after—even in the hour of death—the sad refrain—
    the tune, the voice, the words,
Resumed—the large, calm Lady walks the narrow aisle,
The wailing melody again—the singer in the prison sings:

> *O sight of shame, and pain, and dole!*
> *O fearful thought—a convict Soul!*   1868

BROTHER OF ALL, WITH GENEROUS HAND

(G. P., BURIED FEBRUARY, 1870)

1

*B*ROTHER of all, with generous hand,
    Of thee, pondering on thee, as o'er thy tomb,
    I and my Soul,
A thought to launch in memory of thee,

A burial verse for thee.
What may we chant, O thou within this tomb?
What tablets, pictures, hang for thee, O millionaire?
—The life thou lived'st we know not,
But that thou walk'dst thy years in barter, 'mid the haunts
    of brokers;
Nor heroism thine, nor war, nor glory.

Yet lingering, yearning, joining soul with thine,
If not thy past we chant, we chant the future,
Select, adorn the future.

2

Lo, Soul, the graves of heroes!
The pride of lands—the gratitudes of men,
The statues of the manifold famous dead, Old World and
    New,
The kings, inventors, generals, poets, (stretch wide thy
    vision, Soul,)
The excellent rulers of the races, great discoverers, sailors,
Marble and brass select from them, with pictures, scenes,
(The histories of the lands, the races, bodied there,
In what they've built for, graced and graved,
Monuments to their heroes.)

3

Silent, my Soul,
With drooping lids, as waiting, ponder'd,
Turning from all the samples, all the monuments of
    heroes.

DRUM TAPS . . . .

While through the interior vistas,
Noiseless uprose, phantasmic (as, by night, Auroras of the
    North,)
Lambent tableaux, prophetic, bodiless scenes,
Spiritual projections.

In one, among the city streets, a laborer's home appear'd,
After his day's work done, cleanly, sweet-air'd, the gas-
    light burning,
The carpet swept, and a fire in the cheerful stove.

In one, the sacred parturition scene,
A happy, painless mother birth'd a perfect child.

In one, at a bounteous morning meal,
Sat peaceful parents, with contented sons.

In one, by twos and threes, young people,
Hundreds concentering, walk'd the paths and streets and
    roads,
Toward a tall-domed school.

In one a trio, beautiful,
Grandmother, loving daughter, loving daughter's daugh-
    ter, sat,
Chatting and sewing.

In one, along a suite of noble rooms,
'Mid plenteous books and journals, paintings on the walls,
    fine statuettes,
Were groups of friendly journeymen, mechanics, young
    and old,
Reading, conversing.

All, all the shows of laboring life,
City and country, women's, men's and children's,
Their wants provided for, hued in the sun, and tinged for
    once with joy,
Marriage, the street, the factory, farm, the house-room,
    lodging-room,
Labor and toil, the bath, gymnasium, play-ground, li-
    brary, college,
The student, boy or girl, led forward to be taught;
The sick cared for, the shoeless shod—the orphan father'd
    and mother'd,
The hungry fed, the houseless housed;
(The intentions perfect and divine,
The workings, details, happy human.)

4

O thou within this tomb,
From thee, such scenes—thou stintless, lavish Giver,
Tallying the gifts of Earth—large as the Earth,
Thy name an Earth, with mountains, fields and rivers.
Nor by your streams alone, you rivers,
By you, your banks, Connecticut,
By you, and all your teeming life, Old Thames,
By you, Potomac, laving the ground Washington trod—
    by you Patapsco,
You, Hudson—you, endless Mississippi—not by you
    alone,
But to the high seas launch, my thought, his memory.

[111]

5

Lo, Soul, by this tomb's lambency,
The darkness of the arrogant standards of the world,
With all its flaunting aims, ambitions, pleasures.

(Old, commonplace, and rusty saws,
The rich, the gay, the supercilious, smiled at long,
Now, piercing to the marrow in my bones,
Fused with each drop my heart's blood jets,
Swim in ineffable meaning.)

Lo, Soul, the sphere requireth, portioneth,
To each his share, his measure,
The moderate to the moderate, the ample to the ample.
Lo, Soul, see'st thou not, plain as the sun,
The only real wealth of wealth in generosity,
The only life of life in goodness?   1870

GODS

1

*T*HOUGHT of the Infinite—the All!
Be thou my God.

2

Lover Divine, and Perfect Comrade!
Waiting, content, invisible yet, but certain,
Be thou my God.

3

Thou—thou, the Ideal Man!
Fair, able, beautiful, content, and loving,
Complete in Body, and dilate in Spirit,
Be thou my God.

4

O Death— (for Life has served its turn;)
Opener and usher to the heavenly mansion!
Be thou my God.

5

Aught, aught, of mightiest, best, I see, conceive, or know,
 (To break the stagnant tie—thee, thee to free, O Soul,)
Be thou my God.

6

Or thee, Old Cause, whene'er advancing;
All great Ideas, the races' aspirations,
All that exalts, releases thee, my Soul!
All heroisms, deeds of rapt enthusiasts,
Be ye my Gods!

7

Or Time and Space!
Or shape of Earth, divine and wondrous!
Or shape in I myself—or some fair shape, I, viewing, wor-
    ship,
Or lustrous orb of Sun, or star by night:
Be ye my Gods.   1870

WARBLE FOR LILAC-TIME

*W*ARBLE me now, for joy of Lilac-time,
    Sort me, O tongue and lips, for Nature's sake,
       and sweet life's sake—and death's the
  same as life's,
Souvenirs of earliest summer—bird's eggs, and the first
  berries;
Gather the welcome signs, (as children, with pebbles, or
  stringing shells;)
Put in April and May—the hylas croaking in the ponds—
  the elastic air,
Bees, butterflies, the sparrow with its simple notes,
Blue-bird, and darting swallow—nor forget the high-hole
  flashing his golden wings,
The tranquil sunny haze, the clinging smoke, the vapor,
Spiritual, airy insects, humming on gossamer wings,
Shimmer of waters, with fish in them—the cerulean
  above;
All that is jocund and sparkling—the brooks running,
The maple woods, the crisp February days, and the sugar-
  making;
The robin, where he hops, bright-eyed, brown-breasted,
With musical clear call at sunrise, and again at sunset,
Or flitting among the trees of the apple-orchard, building
  the nest of his mate;
The melted snow of March—the willow sending forth its
  yellow-green sprouts;
—For spring-time is here! the summer is here! and what is
  this in it and from it?

Thou, Soul, unloosen'd—the restlessness after I know not
  what;
Come! let us lag here no longer—let us be up and away!
O for another world! O if one could but fly like a bird!
O to escape—to sail forth, as in a ship!
To glide with thee, O Soul, o'er all, in all, as a ship o'er
  the waters!
—Gathering these hints, these preludes—the blue sky, the
  grass, the morning drops of dew;
(With additional songs—every spring will I now strike up
  additional songs,
Nor ever again forget, these tender days, the chants of
  Death as well as Life;)
The lilac-scent, the bushes, and the dark green, heart-
  shaped leaves,
Wood violets, the little delicate pale blossoms called inno-
  cence,
Samples and sorts not for themselves alone, but for their
  atmosphere,
To tally, drench'd with them, tested by them,
Cities and artificial life, and all their sights and scenes,
My mind henceforth, and all its meditations—my recita-
  tives,
My land, my age, my race, for once to serve in songs,
(Sprouts, tokens ever of death indeed the same as life,)
To grace the bush I love—to sing with the birds,
A warble for joy of Lilac-time.   1870

O STAR OF FRANCE!

1870-71

1

O STAR of France!
    The brightness of thy hope and strength and
        fame,
Like some proud ship that led the fleet so long,
Beseems to-day a wreck, driven by the gale, a mastless
    hulk;
And 'mid its teeming, madden'd, half-drown'd crowds,
Nor helm nor helmsman.

2

Dim, smitten star!
Orb not of France alone—pale symbol of my soul, its dear-
    est hopes,
The struggle and the daring—rage divine for liberty,
Of aspirations towards the far ideal—enthusiast's dreams
    of brotherhood,
Of terror to the tyrant and the priest.

3

Star crucified! by traitors sold!
Star panting o'er a land of death—heroic land!
Strange, passionate, mocking, frivolous land.
Miserable! yet for thy errors, vanities, sins, I will not now
    rebuke thee;
Thy unexampled woes and pangs have quell'd them all,
And left thee sacred.

[116]

In that amid thy many faults, thou ever aimedst highly,
In that thou wouldst not really sell thyself, however great
    the price,
In that thou surely wakedst weeping from thy drugg'd
    sleep,
In that alone, among thy sisters, thou, Giantess, didst rend
    the ones that shamed thee,
In that thou couldst not, wouldst not, wear the usual
    chains,
This cross, thy livid face, thy pierced hands and feet,
The spear thrust in thy side.

4

O star! O ship of France, beat back and baffled long!
Bear up, O smitten orb! O ship, continue on!

Sure, as the ship of all, the Earth itself,
Product of deathly fire and turbulent chaos,
Forth from its spasms of fury and its poisons,
Issuing at last in perfect power and beauty,
Onward, beneath the sun, following its course,
So thee, O ship of France!

Finish'd the days, the clouds dispell'd,
The travail o'er, the long-sought extrication,
When lo! reborn, high o'er the European world,
(In gladness, answering thence, as face afar to face, reflect-
    ing ours, Columbia,)
Again thy star, O France—fair, lustrous star,
In heavenly peace, clearer, more bright than ever,
Shall beam immortal.   1871

TO THEE, OLD CAUSE!

C O thee, old Cause!
    Thou peerless, passionate, good cause!
    Thou stern, remorseless, sweet Idea!
Deathless throughout the ages, races, lands!
After a strange, sad war—great war for thee,
(I think all war through time was really fought, and ever
    will be really fought, for thee;)
These chants for thee—the eternal march of thee.

Thou orb of many orbs!
Thou seething principle! Thou well-kept, latent germ!
    Thou center!
Around the idea of thee the strange sad war revolving,
With all its angry and vehement play of causes,
(With yet unknown results to come, for thrice a thou-
    sand years,)
These recitatives for thee—my Book and the War are one,
Merged in its spirit I and mine—as the contest hinged on
    thee,
As a wheel on its axis turns, this Book, unwitting to itself,
Around the Idea of thee.   1871

FOR HIM I SING

FOR him I sing,
    I raise the Present on the Past,
      (As some perennial tree, out of its roots, the
         present on the past:)
With time and space I him dilate—and fuse the immortal
    laws,
To make himself, by them, the law unto himself.   1871

———

STILL, THOUGH THE ONE I SING

STILL, though the one I sing,
    (One, yet of contradictions made,) I dedicate to
        Nationality,
I leave in him Revolt, (O latent right of insurrection! O
    quenchless, indispensable fire!)   1871

———

THE BASE OF ALL METAPHYSICS

AND now, gentlemen,
    A word I give to remain in your memories and
        minds,
As base, and finale too, for all metaphysics.

(So, to the students, the old professor,
At the close of his crowded course.)
Having studied the new and antique, the Greek and Ger-
    manic systems,

[119]

Kant having studied and stated—Fichte and Schelling and
Hegel,

Stated the lore of Plato—and Socrates, greater than Plato,

And greater than Socrates sought and stated—Christ divine having studied long,

I see reminiscent to-day those Greek and Germanic sys-
tems,

See the philosophies all—Christian churches and tenets
see,

Yet underneath Socrates clearly see—and underneath
Christ the divine I see,

The dear love of man for his comrade—the attraction of
friend to friend,

Of the well-married husband and wife—of children and
parents,

Of city for city, and land for land.   1871

SONG OF THE EXPOSITION

1

*A*FTER all, not to create only, or found only,
    But to bring, perhaps from afar, what is already
        founded,

To give it our own identity, average, limitless, free;

To fill the gross, the torpid bulk with vital religious fire;

Not to repel or destroy, so much as accept, fuse, rehabili-
tate;

To obey, as well as command—to follow, more than to
lead;

These also are the lessons of our New World;
—While how little the New, after all—how much the
    Old, Old World!

Long, long, long, has the grass been growing,
Long and long has the rain been falling,
Long has the globe been rolling round.

2

Come, Muse, migrate from Greece and Ionia;
Cross out, please, those immensely overpaid accounts,
That matter of Troy, and Achilles' wrath, and Eneas',
    Odysseus' wanderings;
Placard *"Removed"* and *"To Let"* on the rocks of your
    snowy Parnassus;
Repeat at Jerusalem—place the notice high on Jaffa's
    gate, and on Mount Moriah;
The same on the walls of your Gothic European Cathe-
    drals, and German, French and Spanish Castles;
For know a better, fresher, busier sphere—a wide, untried
    domain awaits, demands you.

3

Responsive to our summons,
Or rather to her long-nurs'd inclination,
Join'd with an irresistible, natural gravitation,
She comes! this famous female—as was indeed to be ex-
    pected;
(For who, so-ever youthful, 'cute and handsome, would
    wish to stay in mansions such as those,

When offer'd quarters with all the modern improvements,
With all the fun that's going—and all the best society?)

She comes! I hear the rustling of her gown;
I scent the odor of her breath's delicious fragrance;
I mark her step divine—her curious eyes a-turning, roll-
   ing,
Upon this very scene.

The Dame of Dames! can I believe, then,
Those ancient temples classic, and castles strong and feu-
   dalistic, could none of them restrain her?
Nor shades of Virgil and Dante—nor myriad memories,
   poems, old associations, magnetize and hold on to
   her?
But that she's left them all—and *here?*

Yes, if you will allow me to say so,
I, my friends, if you do not, can plainly see Her,
The same Undying Soul of Earth's activity's, beauty's,
   heroism's Expression,
Out from her evolutions hither come—submerged the
   strata of her former themes,
Hidden and cover'd by to-day's—foundation of to-day's;
Ended, deceas'd, through time, her voice by Castaly's
   fountain;
Silent through time the broken-lipp'd Sphinx in Egypt—
   silent those century-baffling tombs;
Closed for aye the epics of Asia's, Europe's helmeted war-
   riors;
Calliope's call forever closed—Clio, Melpomene, Thalia
   closed and dead;

Seal'd the stately rhythmus of Una and Oriana—ended
    the quest of the Holy Graal;
Jerusalem a handful of ashes blown by the wind—extinct;
The Crusaders' streams of shadowy, midnight troops, sped
    with the sunrise;
Amadis, Tancred, utterly gone—Charlemagne, Roland,
    Oliver gone,
Palmerin, ogre, departed—vanish'd the turrets that Usk
    reflected,
Arthur vanish'd with all his knights—Merlin and Lance-
    lot and Galahad—all gone—dissolv'd utterly, like an
    exhalation;
Pass'd! pass'd! for us, forever pass'd! that once so mighty
    World—now void, inanimate, phantom World!
Embroider'd, dazzling World! with all its gorgeous leg-
    ends, myths,
Its kings and barons proud—its priests, and warlike lords,
    and courtly dames;
Pass'd to its charnel vault—laid on the shelf—coffin'd,
    with Crown and Armor on,
Blazon'd with Shakspere's purple page,
And dirged by Tennyson's sweet sad rhyme.

I say I see, my friends, if you do not, the Animus of all
    that World,
Escaped, bequeath'd, vital, fugacious as ever, leaving those
    dead remains, and now this spot approaching, filling;
—And I can hear what may be you do not—a terrible
    æsthetical commotion,
With howling, desperate gulp of "flower" and "bower,"
With "Sonnet to Matilda's Eyebrow" quite, quite frantic;

With gushing, sentimental reading circles turn'd to ice or
    stone;
With many a squeak, (in meter choice,) from Boston,
    New York, Philadelphia, London;
As she, the illustrious Emigré, (having, it is true, in her
    day, although the same, changed, journey'd consider-
    able,)
Making directly for this rendezvous—vigorously clearing
    a path for herself—striding through the confusion,
By thud of machinery and shrill steam-whistle undis-
    may'd,
Bluff'd not a bit by drain-pipe, gasometers, artificial ferti-
    lizers,
Smiling and pleased, with palpable intent to stay,
She's here, install'd amid the kitchen ware!

4

But hold—don't I forget my manners?
To introduce the Stranger (what else indeed have I come
    for?) to thee, Columbia:
In Liberty's name, welcome, Immortal! clasp hands,
And ever henceforth Sisters dear be both.
Fear not, O Muse! truly new ways and days receive, sur-
    round you,
(I candidly confess, a queer, queer race, of novel fashion,)
And yet the same old human race—the same within, with-
    out,
Faces and hearts the same—feelings the same—yearnings
    the same,
The same old love—beauty and use the same.

5

We do not blame thee, Elder World—nor separate our-
selves from thee:
(Would the Son separate himself from the Father?)
Looking back on thee—seeing thee to thy duties, gran-
deurs, through past ages bending, building,
We build to ours to-day.

Mightier than Egypt's tombs,
Fairer than Grecia's, Roma's temples,
Prouder than Milan's statued, spired Cathedral,
More picturesque than Rhenish castle-keeps,
We plan, even now, to raise, beyond them all,
Thy great Cathedral, sacred Industry—no tomb,
A Keep for life for practical Invention.

As in a waking vision,
E'en while I chant, I see it rise—I scan and prophesy out-
side and in,
Its manifold ensemble.

6

Around a Palace,
Loftier, fairer, ampler than any yet,
Earth's modern Wonder, History's Seven outstripping,
High rising tier on tier, with glass and iron façades.
Gladdening the sun and sky—enhued in cheerfulest hues,
Bronz, lilac, robin's-egg, marine and crimson,
Over whose golden roof shall flaunt, beneath thy banner,
Freedom,
The banners of The States, the flags of every land,
A brood of lofty, fair, but lesser Palaces shall cluster.

[125]

DRUM TAPS . . . .

Somewhere within the walls of all,
Shall all that forwards perfect human life be started,
Tried, taught, advanced, visibly exhibited.

Here shall you trace in flowing operation,
In every state of practical, busy movement,
The rills of Civilization.
Materials here, under your eye, shall change their shape,
    as if by magic;
The cotton shall be pick'd almost in the very field,
Shall be dried, clean'd, ginn'd, baled, spun into thread
    and cloth, before you:
You shall see hands at work at all the old processes, and
    all the new ones;
You shall see the various grains, and how flour is made,
    and then bread baked by the bakers;
You shall see the crude ores of California and Nevada
    passing on and on till they become bullion;
You shall watch how the printer sets type, and learn what
    a composing stick is;
You shall mark, in amazement, the Hoe press whirling its
    cylinders, shedding the printed leaves steady and fast:
The photograph, model, watch, pin, nail, shall be created
    before you.

In large calm halls, a stately Museum shall teach you the
    infinite, solemn lessons of Minerals;
In another, woods, plants, Vegetation shall be illustrated
    —in another Animals, animal life and development.
One stately house shall be the Music House;

· · · · · · · · · · · · · · DRUM TAPS

Others for other Arts—Learning, the Sciences, shall all be
    here;
None shall be slighted—none but shall here be honor'd,
    help'd, exampled.

7

This, this and these, America, shall be *your* Pyramids and
    Obelisks,
Your Alexandrian Pharos, gardens of Babylon,
Your temple at Olympia.

The male and female many laboring not,
Shall ever here confront the laboring many,
With precious benefits to both—glory to all,
To thee, America—and thee, Eternal Muse.

And here shall ye inhabit, Powerful Matrons!
In your vast state, vaster than all the old;
Echoed through long, long centuries to come,
To sound of different, prouder songs, with stronger
    themes,
Practical, peaceful life—the people's life—the People
    themselves,
Lifted, illumin'd, bathed in peace—elate, secure in peace.

8

Away with themes of War, away with War itself!
Hence from my shuddering sight, to never more return,
    that show of blacken'd, mutilated corpses!
That hell unpent, and raid of blood—fit for wild tigers,
    or for lop-tongued wolves—not reasoning men!

And in its stead speed Industry's campaigns!
With thy undaunted armies, Engineering!
The pennants, Labor, loosen'd to the breeze!
Thy bugles sounding loud and clear!

Away with old romance!
Away with novels, plots, and plays of foreign courts!
Away with love-verses, sugar'd in rhyme—the intrigues,
    amours of idlers,
Fitted for only banquets of the night, where dancers to
    late music slide;
The unhealthy pleasures, extravagant dissipations of the
    few,
With perfumes, heat and wine, beneath the dazzling chan-
    deliers.

9

To you, ye Reverent, sane Sisters,
To this resplendent day, the present scene,
These eyes and ears that like some broad parterre bloom
    up around, before me,
I raise a voice for far superber themes for poets and for
    Art,
To exalt the present and the real,
To teach the average man the glory of his daily walk and
    trade,
To sing, in songs, how exercise and chemical life are never
    to be baffled;
Boldly to thee, America, to-day! and thee, Immortal
    Muse!
To practical, manual work, for each and all—to plough,
    hoe, dig,

To plant and tend the tree, the berry, the vegetables,
    flowers,
For every man to see to it that he really do something—
    for every woman too;
To use the hammer, and the saw, (rip or cross-cut,)
To cultivate a turn for carpentering, plastering, painting,
To work as tailor, tailoress, nurse, hostler, porter,
To invent a little—something ingenious—to aid the wash-
    ing, cooking, cleaning,
And hold it no disgrace to take a hand at them themselves.

I say I bring thee, Muse, to-day and here,
All occupations, duties broad and close,
Toil, healthy toil and sweat, endless, without cessation,
The old, old general burdens, interests, joys,
The family, parentage, childhood, husband and wife,
The house-comforts—the house itself, and all its belong-
    ings,
Food and its preservations—chemistry applied to it;
Whatever forms the average, strong, complete, sweet-
    blooded Man or Woman—the perfect, longeve Per-
    sonality,
And helps its present life to health and happiness—and
    shapes its Soul,
For the eternal Real Life to come.

With latest materials, works,
Steam-power, the great Express lines, gas, petroleum,
These triumphs of our time, the Atlantic's delicate cable,
The Pacific Railroad, the Suez canal, the Mont Cenis
    tunnel;

[129]

Science advanced, in grandeur and reality, analyzing
    everything,
This world all spann'd with iron rails—with lines of
    steamships threading every sea,
Our own Rondure, the current globe I bring.

10

And thou, high-towering One—America!
Thy swarm of offspring towering high—yet higher thee,
    above all towering,
With Victory on thy left, and at thy right hand Law;
Thou Union, holding all—fusing, absorbing, tolerating
    all,
Thee, ever thee, I bring.

Thou—also thou, a world!
With all thy wide geographies, manifold, different, dis-
    tant,
Rounding by thee in One—one common orbic language,
One common indivisible destiny and Union.

11

And by the spells which ye vouchsafe,
To those, your ministers in earnest,
I here personify and call my themes,
To make them pass before ye.

Behold, America! (And thou, ineffable Guest and Sister!)
For thee come trooping up thy waters and thy lands:
Behold! thy fields and farms, thy far-off woods and moun-
    tains,
As in procession coming.

Behold! the sea itself!
And on its limitless, heaving breast, thy ships:
See! where their white sails, bellying in the wind, speckle
    the green and blue!
See! thy steamers coming and going, steaming in or out
    of port!
See! dusky and undulating, their long pennants of smoke!

Behold, in Oregon, far in the north and west,
Or in Maine, far in the north and east, thy cheerful axe-
    men,
Wielding all day their axes!

Behold, on the lakes, thy pilots at their wheels—thy oars-
    men!
Behold how the ash writhes under those muscular arms!

There by the furnace, and there by the anvil,
Behold thy sturdy blacksmiths, swinging their sledges;
Overhand so steady—overhand they turn and fall, with
    joyous clank,
Like a tumult of laughter.

Behold! (for still the procession moves,)
Behold, Mother of All, thy countless sailors, boatmen,
    coasters!
The myriads of thy young and old mechanics!
Mark—mark the spirit of invention everywhere—thy
    rapid patents,
Thy continual workshops, foundries, risen or rising;
See, from their chimneys, how the tall flame-fires stream!

[131]

Mark, thy interminable farms, North, South,
Thy wealthy Daughter-States, Eastern, and Western,
The varied products of Ohio, Pennsylvania, Missouri,
    Georgia, Texas, and the rest;
Thy limitless crops—grass, wheat, sugar, corn, rice, hemp,
    hops,
Thy barns all fill'd—thy endless freight-trains, and thy
    bulging store-houses,
The grapes that ripen on thy vines—the apples in thy
    orchards,
Thy incalculable lumber, beef, pork, potatoes—thy coal—
    thy gold and silver,
The inexhaustible iron in thy mines.

12

All thine, O sacred Union!
Ship, farm, shop, barns, factories, mines,
City and State—North, South, item and aggregate,
We dedicate, dread Mother, all to thee!

Protectress absolute, thou! Bulwark of all!
For well we know that while thou givest each and all,
    (generous as God,)
Without thee, neither all nor each, nor land, home,
Ship, nor mine—nor any here, this day, secure,
Nor aught, nor any day secure.

13

And thou, thy Emblem, waving over all!
Delicate beauty! a word to thee, (it may be salutary;)

Remember, thou hast not always been, as here to-day, so
    comfortably ensovereign'd;
In other scenes than these have I observ'd thee, flag;
Not quite so trim and whole, and freshly blooming, in
    folds of stainless silk;
But I have seen thee, bunting, to tatters torn, upon thy
    splinter'd staff,
Or clutch'd to some young color-bearer's breast, with des-
    perate hands,
Savagely struggled for, for life or death—fought over long,
'Mid cannon's thunder-crash, and many a curse, and groan
    and yell—and rifle-volleys cracking sharp,
And moving masses, as wild demons surging—and lives as
    nothing risk'd,
For thy mere remnant, grimed with dirt and smoke, and
    sopp'd in blood;
For sake of that, my beauty—and that thou might'st dally,
    as now, secure up there,
Many a good man have I seen go under.

14

Now here, and these, and hence, in peace all thine, O
    Flag!
And here, and hence, for thee, O universal Muse! and
    thou for them!
And here and hence, O Union, all the work and work-
    men thine!
The poets, women, sailors, soldiers, farmers, miners, stu-
    dents thine!
None separate from Thee—henceforth one only, we and
    Thou;

(For the blood of the children—what is it only the blood
    Maternal?
And lives and works—what are they all at last except the
    roads to Faith and Death?)

While we rehearse our measureless wealth, it is for thee,
    dear Mother!
We own it all and several to-day indissoluble in Thee;
—Think not our chant, our show, merely for products
    gross, or lucre—it is for Thee, the Soul, electrical,
    spiritual!
Our farms, inventions, crops, we own in Thee! Cities and
    States in Thee!
Our freedom all in Thee! our very lives in Thee!   1871

ON THE BEACH, AT NIGHT

1

ON the beach, at night,
    Stands a child, with her father,
    Watching the east, the autumn sky.

Up through the darkness,
While ravening clouds, the burial clouds, in black masses
    spreading,
Lower, sullen and fast, athwart and down the sky,
Amid a transparent clear belt of ether yet left in the east,
Ascends, large and calm, the lord-star Jupiter;
And nigh at hand, only a very little above,
Swim the delicate brothers, the Pleiades.

2

From the beach, the child, holding the hand of her father,
Those burial-clouds that lower, victorious, soon to devour
    all,
Watching, silently weeps.

Weep not, child,
Weep not, my darling,
With these kisses let me remove your tears;
The ravening clouds shall not long be victorious,
They shall not long possess the sky—shall devour the
    stars only in apparition:
Jupiter shall emerge—be patient—watch again another
    night—the Pleiades shall emerge,
They are immortal—all those stars, both silvery and
    golden, shall shine out again,
The great stars and the little ones shall shine out again—
    they endure;
The vast immortal suns, and the long-enduring pensive
    moons, shall again shine.

3

Then, dearest child, mournest thou only for Jupiter?
Considerest thou alone the burial of the stars?

Something there is,
(With my lips soothing thee, adding, I whisper,
I give thee the first suggestion, the problem and indirec-
    tion,)
Something there is more immortal even than the stars,

(Many the burials, many the days and nights, passing
  away,)
Something that shall endure longer even than lustrous
  Jupiter,
Longer than sun, or any revolving satellite,
Or the radiant brothers, the Pleiades.   1871

GLIDING O'ER ALL

*G*LIDING o'er all, through all,
    Through Nature, Time, and Space,
    As a ship on the waters advancing,
The voyage of the soul—not life alone,
Death, many deaths I'll sing.   1871

ETHIOPIA SALUTING THE COLORS

(A Reminiscence of 1864)

1

*W*HO are you, dusky woman, so ancient, hardly
        human,
        With your woolly-white and turban'd head,
        and bare bony feet?
Why, rising by the roadside here, do you the colors greet?

2

('Tis while our army lines Carolina's sand and pines,
Forth from thy hovel door, thou, Ethiopia, com'st to me,
As, under doughty Sherman, I march toward the sea.)

[136]

3

Me, master, years a hundred, since from my parents
  sunder'd,
A little child, they caught me as the savage beast is caught;
Then hither me, across the sea, the cruel slaver brought.

4

No further does she say, but lingering all the day,
Her high-borne turban'd head she wags, and rolls her
  darkling eye,
And curtseys to the regiments, the guidons moving by.

5

What is it, fateful woman—so blear, hardly human?
Why wag your head, with turban bound—yellow, red and
  green?
Are the things so strange and marvelous, you see or have
  seen?   1871

DELICATE CLUSTER

DELICATE cluster! flag of teeming life!
  Covering all my lands! all my sea-shores lining!
  Flag of death! (how I watch'd you through the
    smoke of battle pressing!
How I heard you flap and rustle, cloth defiant!)
Flag cerulean! sunny flag! with the orbs of night dappled!
Ah, my silvery beauty! ah, my woolly white and crimson!
Ah, to sing the song of you, my matron mighty!
My sacred one, my mother.   1871

ADIEU TO A SOLDIER

ADIEU, O soldier!
       You of the rude campaigning, (which we
              shared,)
The rapid march, the life of the camp,
The hot contention of opposing fronts—the long ma-
       neuver,
Red battles with their slaughter,—the stimulus—the
       strong, terrific game,
Spell of all brave and manly hearts—the trains of Time
       through you, and like of you, all fill'd,
With war, and war's expression.

Adieu, dear comrade!
Your mission is fulfill'd—but I, more warlike,
Myself, and this contentious soul of mine,
Still on our own campaigning bound,
Through untried roads, with ambushes, opponents lined,
Through many a sharp defeat and many a crisis—often
       baffled,
Here marching, ever marching on, a war fight out—aye,
       here,
To fiercer, weightier battles give expression.   1871

THIS DUST WAS ONCE THE MAN

THIS dust was once the Man,
    Gentle, plain, just and resolute—under whose
      cautious hand,
Against the foulest crime in history known in any land or
    age,
Was saved the Union of These States.   1871